LIVING FESTIVALS

OMNIBUS

CHRISTMAS, SHROVE TUESDAY,
ASH WEDNESDAY AND MARDI GRAS,
HOLY WEEK, EASTER

RMEP

RELIGIOUS AND MORAL EDUCATION PRESS

Religious and Moral Education Press
An imprint of Chansitor Publications Ltd
A Subsidiary Company of Hymns Ancient & Modern Ltd
St Mary's Works, St Mary's Plain
Norwich, Norfolk NR3 3BH

Individual titles first published as separate volumes in the Living
Festivals Series:

Christmas © 1982 Antony Ewens
Shrove Tuesday, Ash Wednesday and Mardi Gras © 1984
    Margaret Davidson
Holy Week © 1984 Norma Fairbairn and Jack Priestley
Easter © 1982 Norma Fairbairn and Jack Priestley

First published in this edition 1991
Reprinted 1994

Printed in Great Britain by BPC Wheatons Ltd, Exeter for
Chansitor Publications Ltd, Norwich

ISBN 0 900274 19 0

Contents

ACKNOWLEDGEMENTS
Illustrations are reproduced by courtesy of:

Barnaby's Picture Library
Camera Press
Mary Evans Picture Library
Express and Echo
The Mansell Collection
Brian and Sally Shuel
Jamie and David Simson
Topham Picture Library

Cover illustration by Jim Lester
Cover design by Andy Jones : Topics Visual Information, Exeter

Christmas
Antony Ewens

Contents

1

Celebrations

Preparing for Christmas

Imagine a house decorated with holly and mistletoe. A fir tree, decked with coloured lights, stands in a prominent position. From its branches hang tinsel, coloured-glass ornaments and a star. At its foot is a pile of brightly-wrapped gifts. Cards are displayed around the room. This scene is repeated in many homes in the weeks before Christmas.

In the streets, in shops and schools too, decorations appear as Christmas approaches. Santa Claus visits the big stores; concerts and parties are held in schools. Children take part in nativity plays, acting the story of the birth of Jesus. Parties of carol singers go from door to door, and carols are heard in churches, chapels and schools.

The postman works long hours, delivering the millions of Christmas cards and gifts which people send to their relations and friends. Shops and stores do brisk business as presents are chosen and wrapped in Christmas paper. Secrecy is all important. Children wait with eager anticipation, wondering what Santa Claus will bring them on 25 December.

At home, preparations are being made in the kitchen for the Christmas meals. Christmas puddings have been made, often each member of the family taking his or her turn to stir the mixture while solemnly making a secret wish. The Christmas cake is being covered with white icing which resembles snow, and is decorated with tiny figures. Mince pies are baked and a turkey is prepared as the main course for the Christmas meal.

Christmas Eve arrives. Children hang stockings at the foot of their beds ready to receive their presents. Late in the evening church services are held so that the birth of Jesus may be celebrated as midnight strikes and Christmas Day begins.

Then Christmas Day itself — the presents are opened and the food eaten. Parties are held and games played. The festival is celebrated.

Two festivals merged into one

A typical British family celebrating Christmas is involved in many customs and traditions. Some are quite modern. Others are linked with the Christian celebration of the birth of Jesus. Many go back to even earlier times, before the birth of Jesus, to an age when people held ceremonies to mark the middle of winter.

Christmas is not a single celebration. It is two festivals merged into one. As time has passed, traditions connected with the midwinter festivities have become mixed with the Christian festival of Jesus' birth.

2

Midwinter Festivals

The winter solstice

For very many years before the birth of Jesus people had held special celebrations at the time of the winter solstice. The word 'solstice' literally means 'the sun standing still'. It does not do that, of course, but the solstices are the days when it is furthest from the Equator. The solstices fall on 21 June and 22 December, and in the northern hemisphere these are the longest and shortest days of the year; in the southern hemisphere the longest and shortest days are the other way around.

When they saw the days getting shorter during the autumn people began to fear that the sun was going away. They believed that by carrying out certain activities they made sure that the sun would return and that plants and crops would grow again.

They hung evergreens in their homes because these plants were living when all else seemed dead. In the Scandinavian countries, Norway, Sweden and Denmark, people believed that the woodland spirits would remain alive in the green leaves in the warmth of their homes. They would then cause the trees and plants to grow again in the spring.

Saturnalia

The ancient Romans held a winter festival called saturnalia. At this feast they honoured Saturn, whom they worshipped as the god of everything that grew. They had a public holiday lasting for a week. People exchanged presents, especially candles, and everyone took part in feasting and games. Slaves were made free for a day, and allowed to do and say what they liked.

Roman Festivities

The sun's birthday
Sun worshippers celebrated 25 December as the sun's birthday. They built bonfires on this day to mark the fact that the amount of sunlight would increase each day. The heat and light of the summer would gradually arrive, causing plants and crops to grow again.

The birth of Jesus
Christians look to Jesus as the founder and head of the church. They believe him to be the Son of God and their saviour.

When Jesus was born, about two thousand years ago, birth certificates were not given and no written records were kept. No one knows the exact date of Jesus' birth. In the early days of Christianity it was decided to celebrate his birthday in midwinter, because this was already an important occasion. The date of 25 December was finally fixed in A.D. 350 by Pope Julius I.

3

Stories

The expectation

For many hundreds of years before Jesus was born, people in Israel had expected the birth of a Messiah, a person sent by God to bring peace and justice to the earth. The prophet Isaiah, in about 720 B.C., wrote:

> *For unto us a child is born, unto us a son is given: and the government shall be upon his shoulder: and his name shall be called Wonderful, Counsellor, The mighty God, The everlasting Father, The Prince of Peace.* (Isaiah 9 : 6.)

When Jesus of Nazareth was born, most people in Israel did not think he was the Messiah Isaiah had spoken of. But those that did gave him the title which in Greek was Christos, or Christ. They became the first *Christ*ians.

Matthew and Luke

The familiar Bible stories of the birth of Jesus are found in Matthew 1 and 2, and Luke 1 and 2. His mother, Mary, learned from an angel that she was to have a baby boy who would be called the Son of God. The child was born in Bethlehem, where Joseph and Mary had gone from their home in Nazareth to be registered. At this time Palestine was ruled by the Romans and the Emperor Augustus had ordered a census, stating that each man must return to his birthplace.

Bethlehem was crowded with people at the time of the census and Joseph and Mary had to take shelter in a stable because there was no room for them in the inn. It was here that Jesus was born and placed in a manger — a feeding-trough for cattle — instead of a cradle.

The infant Jesus was visited by two groups of people. Luke tells us that some shepherds, spending the night on the hillside with their sheep, saw a vision of an angel. The angel told them of the birth of a saviour, Christ the Lord, in Bethlehem. The shepherds ran to the town, where they found the baby lying in a manger, just as the angel had said. The shepherds told Mary and Joseph what the angel had said about the child, then returned to their flocks, praising God because of what they had heard and seen.

Nativity scene

The second group of visitors is described as the Wise Men, the Magi or the Kings. Matthew writes about some men who studied the stars. They travelled to Jerusalem in search of a baby boy, destined to be a king, whose star they had seen. By tradition these men were kings and there were three of them, but Matthew mentions neither of these details. The travellers first approached King Herod, who was cross and anxious when he learned of a new king. Herod's advisers announced that the Messiah was to be born in Bethlehem, so the travellers continued their journey, halting when the star stopped above the stable in Bethlehem. They worshipped the child and gave him gifts of gold, frankincense and myrrh.

Herod had told the travellers to let him know where the new king was so that he also could worship him. But Herod was not to be trusted and the travellers, warned in a dream, went home a different way.

Soon afterwards Joseph took Mary and the child Jesus away to Egypt. They were just in time. Herod, eager to get rid of a possible rival, ordered that all boys in Bethlehem less than two years old were to be put to death. Joseph and his family remained in Egypt until Herod had died.

John

The Gospel of John does not tell the story of Jesus' birth. Instead John thinks about the meaning of his coming. He writes that Jesus is like light coming into the world and shining on mankind. The darkness of human wrongdoing could never put out the light of God's truth which Jesus brought to the earth.

Now we can see a good reason why early Christians in Europe chose to use the winter solstice as a celebration of Christ's birth (literally the Mass of Christ). John described Jesus as light coming into the world. In the winter solstice celebrations, light was the chief symbol. There were fires and torches and the candles of the Roman saturnalia. In Israel, too, there was a festival of light at about the same time. This was the Jewish festival of Chanukah, which is still celebrated and which you can read about in another book in this series. The candles in the Jewish temple represented the truth of what Christians call the Old Testament. Christians thought Jesus was that truth.

4

Symbols

A great many symbols are connected with Christmas. Each of the decorations seen in streets and homes has its own history and meaning. Over the years the meanings of many of the symbols have changed. In particular, the traditions associated with the midwinter festival were often taken over by early Christians and given a new meaning to link them with the birth of Jesus.

Symbols from the midwinter festivals
Evergreens   Evergreen plants originally reminded people that some forms of life continued through the winter, when most of nature appeared to have died. Especially in Scandinavia, homes were decorated with evergreens to ensure that the woodland spirits (who were believed to live in these plants) would survive the winter and cause new growth in the spring. Plants which bear berries were especially popular, since their fruits gave the promise of new life to come.

Mistletoe   Stories were told about the various evergreen plants to explain why they were hung in people's homes. A Scandinavian legend has it that the Norse gods had promised never to hurt Balder, the sun god, because he gave life and warmth to everything. They cast spells on all the things that might have harmed Balder, but unfortunately they forgot the mistletoe. Loki, the god of evil, found out about this and made a sharp arrow from a mistletoe branch. Balder was killed by the arrow but the other gods brought him to life again and the mistletoe promised that it would never again harm anyone.

Mistletoe therefore became a symbol of love. When Christians took over the tradition of hanging mistletoe in their homes they introduced the custom of kissing beneath it. This reminded them of Jesus' teaching that his followers should love one another because their god was a god of love.

Holly Holly was often hung in homes at the time of the midwinter festival. Later, as a Christian symbol, it acquired meanings associated with the birth and death of Jesus. The Christmas carol *The Holly and the Ivy* gives examples of this.

THE HOLLY AND THE IVY

The holly and the ivy,
When they are both full grown,
Of all the trees that are in the wood,
The holly bears the crown:

chorus: *The rising of the sun*
And the running of the deer,
The playing of the merry organ,
Sweet singing in the choir.

The holly bears a blossom,
As white as the lily flower,
And Mary bore sweet Jesus Christ,
To be our sweet Saviour:

The holly bears a berry,
As red as any blood,
And Mary bore sweet Jesus Christ,
To do poor sinners good:

The holly bears a prickle,
As sharp as any thorn,
And Mary bore sweet Jesus Christ,
On Christmas day in the morn:

The holly bears a bark,
As bitter as any gall,
And Mary bore sweet Jesus Christ,
For to redeem us all:

The holly's white flower represents the purity of Mary; its prickly leaves remind us of the crown of thorns placed on Jesus' head before he was crucified; its red berries are the drops of blood which came when the thorns pricked him; its bark, 'as bitter as any gall', represents the bitterness of Jesus' suffering on the cross.

The modern Scandinavian name for the holly tree is the Christ-thorn; the English name 'holly' probably came from the word 'holy'.

An American custom which is sometimes copied in Britain is that of hanging a holly wreath on a door or window.

The fir tree Fir trees were an important feature of the celebrations at the midwinter festival because, like the holly and the mistletoe, they were evergreens. There is a story which explains how the fir tree became a Christian symbol — the Christmas tree.

In the eighth century an Englishman from Crediton in Devon, called Winfrith (later known as St Boniface), went to Germany to spread the Christian faith. By now, Christians had adopted many ancient traditions in their Christmas celebrations. However, there were some customs which Christians wanted to stop because the practices were cruel or wicked. One of these was the sacrifice of animals — or sometimes people — to a god.

One December Boniface discovered a group of people standing beneath an oak tree. They were on the point of sacrificing a young child to a pagan god. The people believed that the sacrifice would please the god so that he would bring them good fortune.

Boniface rescued the child and had the oak chopped down. At its foot was a small fir tree. Boniface gave this to the people as a holy symbol. Its evergreen leaves he described as a symbol of eternal life. He gave the fir the name 'Tree of the Christ-child'.

The Christmas tree continued as a tradition in Germany. Many years after the death of Boniface a famous Christian, Martin Luther, decorated a fir tree with candles to represent Jesus as the Light of the World.

It was not until the middle of the nineteenth century that the Christmas tree was introduced into Britain by Queen Victoria's husband, the German-born Prince Albert. The lighted tree remains a symbol of Jesus, the Light of the World.

Tree decorations In pre-Christian times there was a custom of hanging brightly painted apples on the branches of trees in

Christmas tree in Trafalgar Square

Christmas

honour of the god Woden. People hoped that this would please Woden so that he would grant a plentiful harvest in the following year.

Glass ornaments are the modern equivalent of the apples, although they do not have any particular meaning nowadays.

The yule-log The ancient European custom of lighting the yule-log was a very important midwinter tradition. A special large log was cut from a fruit-bearing tree, such as the apple, and placed on the fire. A glass of wine was poured on the log, and the head of the family set fire to it, using the remains of the previous year's yule-log to get the fire going. The fire burned for a number of days to celebrate the return of the sun following the shortest day of the year.

Wassailing The custom of wassailing consisted of singing songs, drinking toasts and making offerings of wine to pagan spirits in the hope that this would lead to a plentiful fruit

Farmers shoot guns into the trees — a wassailing custom

harvest. The word 'wassail' comes from Anglo-Saxon words (waes haeil) which mean 'good health to you'. Until quite recent times wassailing was a common custom in rural Britain and farmers would sometimes fire guns into the branches of the fruit trees to frighten away evil spirits. Some of the wassailing traditions have been taken over and merged with the custom of carol singing around the streets.

Christian symbols
A number of Christmas traditions have been developed by Christians. Some of them have links with pre-Christian customs, others are completely original.

Symbols connected with the tree   The practice of decorating the Christmas tree with a star is a reminder of the star which led the travellers to the birthplace of Jesus.

Sometimes a doll is placed at the top of the tree. Originally this was supposed to represent the baby Jesus or the Angel Gabriel but nowadays the doll is often dressed as a fairy or a princess!

A legend is told to explain the origin of tinsel. A poor woman worked hard to provide for her family. One night some spiders spun their webs on the family's Christmas tree and as a reward for the woman's goodness, the Christ-child turned the webs to silver. Tinsel is supposed to represent the silver webs.

Symbols connected with light   We have seen that the symbol of light is important in the celebration of Christ's birth because Christians regard Jesus as the Light of the World. The candles or lights on the tree remind us of this. In many churches an Advent ring can be seen. This consists of four candles in a ring with a fifth candle in the centre. The candles are lighted, one by one, on the four Sundays during Advent (the period before Christmas when Jesus' coming is awaited), the final candle being lighted on Christmas morning. The Advent ring symbolizes the light of Jesus coming into the world.

Christmas

A Scandinavian custom, now widely practised in Britain, is Christingle. The Christingle is an orange, representing the world, into which is placed a candle symbolizing Jesus, the Light of the World. At Christingle services each child in the church is presented with a Christingle.

Christingle orange

The Crib The custom of making a Christmas crib is widespread. In many churches, and elsewhere, a model of the Christ-child in the manger is made, together with figures representing Mary and Joseph, the shepherds and Wise Men and the animals which are supposed to have inhabited the stable. Mince pies are thought to have originated as tiny replicas of Jesus' crib.

Plays In times before most people could read, Bible stories were presented to the general public in the form of plays, usually known as miracle plays. Nativity plays, often performed in schools at Christmas, continue this tradition.

Another custom, not Christian in origin, is that of mummers' plays. In these plays, based on the theme of good versus evil, the actors dress in costumes, with masks, to portray scenes such as St George killing the dragon or the story of Robin Hood. The action usually includes a sword dance in which the victim nearly dies and is restored by the doctor, a visit by Beelzebub the devil, and a good deal of clowning. The words of the plays were passed on by mouth, never written down, so much variation occurred.

In more recent years pantomimes have become the traditional type of play performed around Christmas time.

Giving — presents and cards　In Chapter 2 it states that at the Roman festival called saturnalia people exchanged presents. As their empire spread, so the Romans took this custom with them. Because saturnalia marked the beginning of new year, in most countries presents are given on New Year's Day, not Christmas Day. In English-speaking and German-speaking countries, however, presents are exchanged on Christmas Day, commemorating the gifts given to Jesus by the Wise Men, although in much of Scotland, for example, the old custom continues.

The sending of Christmas cards is a recent development,

An early Christmas card

Christmas

dating from 1843. In that year Sir Henry Cole made a card for John C. Horsley. It was entitled 'Brimming Cheer' and showed a family celebrating Christmas and also giving gifts of food and clothing to the poor. This card, believed to be the first Christmas card, may be seen in London at the Victoria and Albert Museum. Before 1843 New Year cards had been sent but nowadays millions of Christmas cards are exchanged, many of them bearing the same words as the first one — 'A Merry Christmas and a Happy New Year to you'.

Santa Claus   The original Santa Claus was St Nicolas, Bishop of Myra in Asia in the fourth century. He was famous for his generosity, which is why he became associated with the giving of presents.

The tradition of St Nicolas was taken to Holland by Dutch sailors. In Holland Sinter Klaas (as they call him) is thought of as a bearded man on a white horse, who brings presents for good children on 6 December (St Nicolas' Day) and a bunch of birch rods for naughty boys and girls.

When the tradition spread to America in the nineteenth century, Santa's character changed. American children thought that he came from the North Pole, so he needed a sledge and reindeer.

We in Britain have acquired our picture of Santa Claus from the Americans. Like them, we celebrate his visit, bringing gifts, on 25 December, Christmas Day itself.

5

Christmas in Other Lands

To write about the Christmas celebrations throughout the world would require a larger book than this. However, it is interesting to compare our familiar customs with those in a few other countries in Europe.

Holland
In Holland activity begins on the last Saturday in November, when St Nicolas arrives in Amsterdam with Black Peter, his servant, who carries a sack of presents and some birch rods. Then St Nicolas, dressed in his bishop's robe and mitre, rides on a white horse to the royal palace, ready to distribute gifts on 6 December.

Austria
In Austria St Nicolas visits children on 6 December, accompanied by the devil. He asks children if they have been good. The devil tries to hit the naughty ones but Nicolas chases him away. If the children promise to be good, Nicolas gives them fruit, nuts and sweets.

Another tradition in Austria is the ceremony of 'showing the Christ-child'. In this, a manger is carried from house to house while carols are sung.

Czechoslovakia
In Czechoslovakia the celebrations continue for a whole month, from 6 December to 6 January. On the first day of the

festivities St Nicolas comes from the sky, accompanied by an angel carrying presents, and by the devil carrying wooden canes. When the children hear them coming they rush to the dining table and start to say their prayers. Children who have been good and who can say the prayers correctly receive presents.

St Nicolas

Another Czech custom is the legend of the golden pigs. Christians in Czechoslovakia, and some other countries, fast at Christmas time. 'Fasting' means that they go without food for part of Christmas Eve and spend time thinking about the meaning of the birth of Jesus. Czech children were told that, if they fasted faithfully, they would see golden pigs on the wall at suppertime. It is said that, when the traditional meal of a small pig was served, the candles cast the shadow of the pig on to the walls and ceiling. At the meal, one chair was left empty for the Christ-child.

Scandinavia

The Christmas festivities in Scandinavia also last for a month, from St Lucia's Day (13 December) to St Knut's Day (13 January).

St Lucia was a Christian martyr put to death in the fourth century. The Vikings imagined her as a shining figure crowned with haloes of light. Nowadays, on St Lucia's Day, the daughter of the family serves coffee and Lucia buns. She wears white and on her head is a crown of evergreens and some lighted candles.

St Knut was a Scandinavian king of the eleventh century. He was made a saint because he was pious and gave generously to the poor. On St Knut's Day the Christmas-tree lights are lit for the last time.

In the Mediterranean countries of Southern Europe and parts of North Africa like Ethiopia, Christmas is celebrated on 6 January. It is not a very important occasion, since Christians in those lands regard Easter as by far the most significant festival of the Christian year.

6

The Meaning of Christmas

The midwinter festivals were times of feasting and enjoyment. Early Christians often took part in them, although they did not believe in a sun god or woodland spirits. Christians abandoned some parts of the festivities — for example, the sacrifice of people and animals — which they believed were wrong. However, they still decorated their homes with evergreens, joined in feasting and exchanged gifts.

As the years passed, new meanings were given to the midwinter customs, meanings which linked them with the birth of Jesus, helping people to understand who Jesus was. The mistletoe became a symbol of God's love; the leaves and berries of the holly represented the suffering of Jesus on the cross.

The main reason for holding a midwinter festival had been people's concern about the shortening days in autumn and early winter. In pre-Christian times, men believed that if they held a feast in honour of the gods, the gods would be pleased and would make the sun shine for longer each day. The light would increase and summer would come again.

Early Christians thought about the idea of light and used it as a symbol to explain the meaning of Jesus' birth. In his Gospel John writes that the birth of Jesus is like light coming into the world. The world is full of the darkness of human wrongdoing but the truth of Jesus shines in that darkness. 'The light shines in the dark and the darkness has never put it out.'

(John 1: 5; *Good News Bible*). At Christmas the early Christians began to think of the light that Jesus brought to earth rather than the light of the sun. This change of thinking took place very slowly.

Early Christians wanted to say more about Jesus, to explain who he was. They soon came to believe that Jesus was God's way of communicating with people. The writer of a Letter to the Hebrews, in the New Testament wrote: 'In the past, God spoke to our ancestors many times and in many ways through the prophets, but in these last days he has spoken to us through his Son.' (Hebrews 1:1, 2a; *Good News Bible*).

The prophets were God's messengers who had passed on God's words to the people, but Jesus, Christians believe, was God himself born as a human being to en*light*en the world.

Previously God had been known as 'The Word'. He had spoken; people had heard. Now suddenly he was seen, as clearly as a light in a dark place. The Word had become flesh. This is how John's Gospel begins.

1 In the beginning was the Word, and the Word was with God, and the Word was God.
2 The same was in the beginning with God.
3 All things were made by him; and without him was not anything made that was made.
4 In him was life; and the life was the light of men.
5 And the light shineth in darkness; and the darkness comprehended it not. (John I: 1-5)

Shrove Tuesday, Ash Wednesday and Mardi Gras

Margaret Davidson

Contents

Fancy dress is worn at the annual pancake race, Chudleigh, Devon

Shrove Tuesday

Introduction

Have you ever heard the phrase 'to have a last fling'? It means to go out and enjoy yourself, perhaps even to do something outrageous or silly before you have to settle down and act responsibly. People have 'a last fling' on the final night of their holiday before they go home or back to work. We might also have 'a last fling' before getting down to work for an examination.

Every year in the Christian world there is a 'last fling' festival – a day of fun and games which comes before a long period of quiet, serious (and sometimes solemn) reflection. This period, of about six weeks, is called Lent.

During Lent, Christians try to remember the forty days of fasting which Jesus spent in the wilderness. Lent always starts on a Wednesday and continues for the next six weeks. Sundays are not included as the traditional 'fast' was lifted on these days. Thus, from the first Wednesday in Lent (Ash Wednesday) to the final Saturday, a period of forty days, many Christians try to live more simply.

The day before Lent starts, Shrove Tuesday, or Pancake Day as we popularly know it, has traditionally been a day for a 'final fling'. On this day Christians ate up all the food that would not keep through Lent and made it a day of feasting. In France and elsewhere it is called Mardi Gras (Fat Tuesday) and in many parts of the world it has become a day of merriment and celebration.

This book is all about the feasting of Shrove Tuesday and the fasting that begins on Ash Wednesday.

1

Shrove Tuesday

Many people talk about Shrove Tuesday without knowing what the word 'Shrove' means. It is not a word we use much today but it was familiar to everyone in the Middle Ages. To understand it we need to look at the period called Lent in the Christian calendar.

Lent lasts for forty days and nights and represents the time that Jesus spent in the desert before he began his teaching. During that time he survived on very little food, concentrating all his thoughts on God. When Christians remembered this event in the life of Jesus they, too, wanted to concentrate on God and put the luxuries of life to one side. For this reason Lent became a time of fasting. Of course, it wasn't possible for people to go without food altogether so they tried to eat as simply as they could. Today, this custom is continued when Christians give up a luxury for Lent.

To make sure they were not tempted, people tried to use up all their rich foods before Lent began on Ash Wednesday. Luxuries of the past may not be considered as luxuries today: they included meat, eggs, milk and fine flour. These were used up to make a feast before the serious Lenten fast began. We can see why the French call it 'Fat Tuesday'.

It was also very important that people should begin Lent in the right frame of mind. Most people went to church to confess their sins to the priest. Afterwards they were considered to be 'shriven' or free from sin. This meant that they could begin Lent with a pure spirit. It was for this reason that, in Britain, the day became known as Shrove Tuesday.

Shrove Tuesday, then, became a feast day when eggs, butter and flour had to be used up. What better way could there be than to make delicious, sizzling-hot pancakes? These were

The Westminster School Pancake Greaze. This famous annual event has been performed for hundreds of years. Traditionally the pancake is brought into school at 11 a.m. in solemn procession. The school cook then attempts to toss the pancake over the 'pancake bar' set high in the ceiling. Waiting boys in fancy dress then fight for the cake in a melee known as the 'greaze'. The boy with the largest portion wins a prize while a half holiday is granted to the whole school.

very popular indeed and soon became a traditional part of the Shrove Tuesday celebrations. In many places the tossing of pancakes while they were being cooked developed into a game. Everybody had to cook, toss and then eat their own pancake. Some people weren't too good at tossing but even if their pancake fell in the fire they still had to eat it!

In another game everyone was expected to eat one pancake before the next one cooked. Unfortunately, pancakes cook very quickly and someone was always left with a piece of very hot pancake when the next one was ready. Their 'punishment' was to be thrown in the nearest gooseberry bush. No doubt the thought of this helped some people to eat very quickly indeed!

Shrove Tuesday began as a preparation for Lent, as we have seen. Gradually, though, fasting became a much less important part of Lent. People might have given up the fast but they were not so willing to give up the feast, and Shrove Tuesday had become firmly fixed as a special day of enjoyment. A number of local customs grew up around it and many of them continue today. In times when there were no televisions, radios, or cinemas people had to entertain themselves and they kept old traditions alive and lively!

Pancake tossing

Tossing pancakes can be a very tricky business but try doing it on the run! In the town of Olney in Buckinghamshire there is a pancake race every Shrove Tuesday. Each contestant has to carry a frying-pan and keep tossing a pancake while running. First held in 1445, the Olney race is open to housewives, who must wear an apron and a scarf or hat. Pancakes have to be tossed three times during the race, which ends at the door of the church. The winner and runner-up each receive a prayer-book as a prize.

Similar races take place in other towns. Sometimes the fun of the race is put to good use, perhaps a sponsored race for charity. To add to the fun fancy dress is often worn.

Women in headscarves and aprons line up for the Olney pancake race

Shrovetide football

Football (soccer) is a game with rigid rules and special positions for each of the players. But it wasn't always like that. It used to be a very wild, rough game with very few rules and anyone could join in. This meant that the teams could be huge with a pitch big enough to take them all. In some places the 'pitch' included the whole parish! Players took the game very seriously and more often than not the match ended with fists and feet flying. This is the type of football match that was often played on Shrove Tuesday.

In the early sixteenth century such a game of football was held every year in the city of Chester. It was the custom for the

Shoemakers Company to present a football to the Drapers Company before the game began. The contest was a very violent affair and old records tell us that many people suffered broken limbs while some were actually in danger of losing their lives. Eventually it was realized that the game was far too dangerous and it had to be stopped. At first people wanted to keep the Shrove Tuesday game so an alternative had to be found. The football was replaced by six silver coins and races were organized in the streets. The silver coins were given as prizes to the winners.

Not all of the Shrove Tuesday football matches disappeared. They are still played today in the towns of Sedgefield, Alnwick, Atherstone and Ashbourne. In Ashbourne, Derbyshire, the game is played on both Shrove Tuesday and Ash Wednesday. It starts at two o'clock in the afternoon and is played on a pitch five kilometres long! In fact, it isn't really a

The ball used at the Sedgefield game: 'When with pancakes you are sated, Come to this ring where you'll be mated, There this ball will be uncast. May this game be better than the last'.

Shrove Tuesday

pitch at all but open countryside with a wide stream, called Henmore Brook, and several smaller streams running across it.

The two teams are made up of as many people as want to play. They are known as Up'ards or Down'ards according to whether the team members come from the north or the south of Henmore Brook. Very few goals are scored and by the end of the game the players are totally exhausted and soaked to the skin after racing backwards and forwards over rough country and through streams.

At Atherstone the game is played in the main street. Although this might sound easier for the players than the Ashbourne game it is particularly tiring because the ball is very, very heavy. Before the game it is filled with water so that no one can kick it very far. Nevertheless, every year on Shrove Tuesday, there are plenty of people who want to play. The winner is the person who manages to 'capture' the ball at the end of three hours' play.

Crowds fight for the ball in the Sedgefield game

Skipping

About two hundred years ago a very strange Shrove Tuesday custom began in the Yorkshire seaside town of Scarborough. People gathered in front of the town hall and after a signal given by the Lord Mayor they began to skip. No one really knows how this began and it is probably one of the most unusual Shrove Tuesday celebrations of all.

Over the years the site of the skipping has moved several times. It began in front of the town hall but was later held in one of the larger parks in Scarborough. Today, everyone meets on the beach. This isn't just a celebration for the young – men, women and children appear on the beach every Shrove Tuesday.

All of these celebrations became part of Shrove Tuesday. They are very enjoyable in themselves but we have to remember that they also have a serious aspect. They all mark a time of preparation and, while people enjoy themselves, some at least are also looking forward to a time of self-denial which will begin on Ash Wednesday.

We must remember, too, that Shrove Tuesday is a day for people to look at themselves and to acknowledge their faults so that they can enter the period of Lent in the right frame of mind. The practice of cleansing described at the beginning of this chapter was not intended to be an easy way of forgetting sins. It brought people to an awareness of the sins they had committed and made them examine carefully the reasons for those sins. When they could do this honestly they were better able to meet the demands of Ash Wednesday.

The festivities of Shrove Tuesday served to bring members of a community together so that this time of self-examination could be shared by all. It came to be a very personal experience and also an experience for the whole Christian community.

2

Mardi Gras

Mardi Gras in France

Shrove Tuesday is celebrated in most European countries. In France it is known as Mardi Gras, which as we have seen means 'Fat Tuesday'.

The reason for this strange name lies not only in the tradition of using up all the fats but also in the custom of leading a well-fattened cow through the streets. No one is really sure when this began but it was probably part of an ancient spring festival. When Christianity came to France converts were probably reluctant to give up all their ancient festivities. The cow became a part of the new religious festival, a symbol of all the luxuries which people would give up during Lent.

Today the cow usually heads the parade through the streets, with townspeople joining in. Sometimes they wear traditional costumes or fancy dress to add to the festivities.

Mardi Gras in New Orleans

In the eighteenth and nineteenth centuries many people emigrated from France to America taking their traditional customs with them. Mardi Gras became firmly established in the Deep South of the United States, especially around New Orleans. At first it was probably very much like Mardi Gras in France but it soon became a carnival.

Not everyone in the area was French and local influences gradually began to appear. The people who had the greatest effect on Mardi Gras were probably the negro slaves and their descendants. They used the carnival to display their own particular form of music and soon this became an important part of Mardi Gras. From it jazz music gradually developed and now the celebrations could almost be mistaken for a jazz festival.

However, everyone joins in the fun, and fancy dress plays a big part in the Mardi Gras parade, which attracts people from all over the world. Local groups, schools, unions and trade committees compete with each other to produce the best decorated floats and costumes. On Mardi Gras they all meet to parade through streets crowded with local people and tourists. As the floats pass by, people on them throw tokens into the watching crowds. These are usually strings of cheap, brightly coloured beads and plastic coins bearing the name of the group of people responsible for the float.

Crowds at Mardi Gras in New Orleans

Shrove Tuesday

Mardi Gras in the West Indies

French people also settled in the West Indies and carried the Mardi Gras festivities there. At first it was celebrated only by the French but it took on a local flavour when the participants began to dress up as their own slaves and servants.

This changeover of roles is a common theme in many festivals. At the Roman feast of Saturnalia master and slave would change places for the day. This also happened at the Feast of Fools in medieval England, and a remnant of the custom is still found in some British regiments where officers serve their men Christmas dinner.

Perhaps this theme is echoed in the New Testament where Jesus, before his crucifixion, is mocked as a king who is humbled and must die.

In 1833 slavery was abolished in the West Indies and so Mardi Gras became a festival of a newly freed people. At first they copied their former masters by dressing with exaggerated finery, but later festivals included figures dressed as characters from stories the slaves had brought from Africa. During the present festivities any fancy dress is acceptable and, especially in Trinidad and Tobago, the carnival has become a fantastic spectacle with thousands joining in.

In Trinidad and Tobago Mardi Gras lasts over the two days before Ash Wednesday, with Shrove Tuesday celebrations forming the climax. The carnival is very carefully timetabled and different types of fancy dress are paraded at separate times.

Everyone who wants to join in starts to plan his or her costume as soon as Christmas is over. Some costumes are cheaply made but others have become so brilliant and ingenious that they are very expensive indeed. Groups of people work together and, during the parade, are often led by a steel band. Each group has a king, queen and courtiers who must be properly dressed. Wood, wire, plastic, metal, velvet, beads and feathers are among the things used to make costumes. By the time Mardi Gras arrives there are as many as a hundred thousand people with specially made costumes.

A fantastic costume made for the Trinidad Carnival

At dawn on Carnival Monday the first sounds are heard. People taking part shout 'Jouvay', which means 'daybreak', and the parade begins. The streets are suddenly filled with people dressed as witches, ghosts and devils, making weird and chilling noises. These sounds are soon drowned as traditional steel bands begin to play. Their own special music, which is now familiar to people all over the world, becomes the only sound to be heard over the crowds in the streets. Steel bands playing calypsos are now as much a part of Mardi Gras as fancy dress.

As the eerie Jouvay characters flood through the streets they are immediately followed by people in traditional costumes. These costumes change little from year to year and are often passed down through families. Clowns, devils, cowboys and dames flow through the streets dancing to the beat of the steel bands. The devils wear bright red, close-fitting clothes with long tails. They dance around the Beast, a fantastic creature with the head of a dragon and a scaly body of metallic green and silver. The whole band is led by Satan or King Lucifer, who has a huge horned head and flowing robes.

Next in the parade comes a crowd of figures from history. The twirling, shifting mass of colour may be made up of Romans, Vikings, Egyptians, Aztecs; in fact nearly everyone in history is represented.

Next in line come the most fabulous costumes of the whole carnival. These are original costumes which are intended to display the talents of the designer. They are often the most expensive to be found. Shifting, shining colours swirl through

The glittering Fire Bird

Samba dancers in the carnival at Rio

Shrove Tuesday

the streets to the never-ending throb of the steel bands. St George and the Dragon, with the dragon forming part of St George's costume, leap and dance alongside the God of Paradise. Close by, the shimmering tail feathers of a Fire Bird lash out towards the King of the Sea.

From dawn to dusk this seething crowd dances and sings its way through the streets, drawing people from the watching crowd along with it. As dusk approaches, prizes are given for the finest costumes and the best steel bands. Singing and dancing continue long into the night as fireworks burst and sparkle across the sky.

The best costumes are awarded prizes

A policeman is confronted by a fantastic creature in the Trinidad festival

Shrove Tuesday

On the second day, Mardi Gras proper, an even greater display takes place. This time the winning costumes are given pride of place at the head of the procession. Everyone dances and sings to the music, usually in a shuffling, stamping style of their own. Every so often, though, a special set of steps begins to emerge and fantastic characters leap and twist in the air. Mardi Gras then draws to an end with dances and picnics in the open air.

Mardi Gras in Trinidad, Tobago, New Orleans and Rio de Janeiro has become one of the most colourful ways of celebrating this festival anywhere in the world. It is easy to forget in the face of carnival that a deeply religious side exists. This is still a time of preparation for Lent and throughout the celebrations this is remembered by all the Christian participants.

Just as Shrove Tuesday in Britain is a time when the community comes together in celebration so, too, is Mardi Gras. Trinidad and Tobago have very mixed communities and visitors from all over the world go to see the carnival. This brings together people of every class, colour, race and belief. It breaks through these differences and includes everyone, young and old, in the spirit of the carnival.

3

Ash Wednesday

After the gaiety of Shrove Tuesday there follows Ash Wednesday, a much more solemn event. In some countries where Mardi Gras is celebrated, a straw effigy representing the carnival is buried in the ground to show that the festivities are over and a new, more serious mood is taken on.

The name Ash Wednesday comes from an ancient custom which originated in the Roman Catholic Church. As you will remember, people were 'shriven' or cleansed of sin on Shrove Tuesday as a preparation for Lent. However, public sinners or people guilty of serious sins and immoral acts were told to return to church on Ash Wednesday.

Early on Ash Wednesday palm crosses given out on Palm Sunday of the previous year were burned and blessed by the priest. Then each of the sinners was marked with ash on the forehead, in the shape of the cross. They were then given a hair shirt to wear and were told that they could not re-enter the church until Holy Tuesday, three days before Good Friday.

During this period from Ash Wednesday to Holy Tuesday each of the sinners was given penance to do. This might include living away from their family, possibly in a monastery, where they would pray, do hard manual labour and acts of charity. Through this the sinners were properly prepared to join in the observance of Holy Week and celebration of Easter.

Shrove Tuesday

Palm cross

The use of ashes as a sign of penitence and sorrow is a very old custom. It is often mentioned in the Old Testament and was a firm part of Jewish tradition. Christ, himself, also referred to this custom and this is recorded in the Gospel according to Matthew 4:21. The Church seems to have accepted this from Jewish tradition and tried to preserve its original meaning.

Later on, many devout Christians began to see penance as a means of preparing themselves for Easter, the most important festival in the Christian calendar. Many of them began to submit to the ceremony of ashes and its accompanying penance voluntarily. By the end of the eleventh century this had become a very widespread custom throughout Europe.

The imposition of ashes continued to be an important event in the Church until the Reformation. Then, many Protestant churches dropped the practice, although the Church of England kept it alive until the seventeenth century. Today, the ceremony is not very common although, in some churches, it has been revived in recent years in a slightly different form.

In the church the altar is draped with a violet altar cloth which remains in place throughout most of Lent. It serves as a constant reminder to those who are observing Lent.

Ash Wednesday has continued to be an important day for Christians. It marks the beginning of Lent, a period of fasting and prayer, in which individuals try to approach Palm Sunday and Good Friday in a serious frame of mind. The forty days of fasting which occur in Lent (Sundays do not count as fast days) are also a reminder of the temptation of Christ in the wilderness and his triumph over it. In the same way, Christians make a positive effort to resist the temptations of everyday life which might lead them astray from the right spirit which is needed for the observance of Holy Week and the celebration of Easter.

4

Feasting and Fasting

Fasting is very common throughout the world and often occurs before important festivals (see the book in this series *Ramadan and Id-ul-Fitr*). Among Christians, fasting is not observed in the same way by all people. In Eastern Europe members of the Orthodox Church observe the fast of Lent in the way it has been observed for many centuries. In Western Christianity Roman Catholics take it more seriously than Protestants though not as seriously as they used to.

There is no single reason why people fast and it may seem a strange custom to those who have never fasted. To understand fasting during Lent we must look at the meanings it has for Christians. As we have seen, fasting is a form of self-denial which is closely linked to the self-denial of Jesus Christ in the wilderness. He denied himself food in order to concentrate his thoughts on God. In the same way Christians hope, during Lent, to become closer to God and at the same time become more aware of their own responsibilities in the world.

Alongside this, Christians feel that fasting is important because it emphasizes the meaning and enjoyment of feast days. It is impossible to appreciate the special meaning of feasts if feasting occurs all the time. Fasting makes life richer because it helps people to enjoy little things and increases the pleasure of feasting. Today, many people think that this sort of pleasure has been lost in many ways. Once, for example, we had mince-pies and turkey only at Christmas. They were a special treat which underlined the special nature of Christmas. Now we can have these things at any time and they no longer seem so special. In Trinidad and Tobago many people are poor and the lengthy preparations for Mardi Gras are often the result of great sacrifices. People work hard to produce costumes and looking forward to the carnival creates great excitement. When Mardi Gras comes this means that it is celebrated to the full.

Many Christians feel that fasting also demonstrates that they have freedom. They are not slaves to habit but are able to control what they do. Often if we like doing something it becomes a habit which we can't stop. Then we have lost our freedom. Smoking and drinking may start as a way of gaining pleasure but can become habits which are very hard to break. Christians often claim that fasting shows that they do have control and then pleasures become real pleasures and not just habits.

Lastly, fasting can be used to develop an understanding of what it is like for those who have no pleasures or indeed do not have basic necessities. Someone who understands this is in a much better position to give help in the best and most useful way.

Shrove Tuesday and Ash Wednesday contrast with each other as a time of feasting and fasting. This contrast gives Christians a better understanding of the observance of Lent and the demands it makes on the individual believer.

Holy Week

Norma Fairbairn and Jack Priestley

Contents

Introduction

Strictly speaking, the week which we call Holy Week is not a festival. The word 'festival' really means 'feast day'. Holy Week comes at the end of the long period of Lent, which is just the opposite of a feast, a fast. It also comes just before the great festival of Easter and it is impossible to understand Easter without knowing about Holy Week. It is a very special week and has been so for nearly two thousand years.

If we look very carefully at the books in the New Testament called the Gospels, which tell us about the life of Jesus of Nazareth, we notice something very strange. Jesus lived for about thirty-three years. He probably spent about three of those years teaching and preaching. But the Gospel writers, Matthew, Mark, Luke and John, use up about one-third of their story to tell us what happened during just one week of those three years. For them it was the most important week in history. We should not be surprised, then, that Christians have always celebrated this week as something special. This is the week we call Holy Week.

1

A Week of Drama

Holy Week is the week before Easter. It has had that name for at least 1600 years. Before that it was called Great Week because, as one early Christian saint, John Chrysostom, said, 'Great deeds were done in it'.

Holy Week is one of the oldest celebrations in Christianity. Christians took notice of it long before they made Christmas an important festival. The way in which it is remembered has hardly changed at all since the very beginning.

A passion-play

Holy Week is a drama. Often it is celebrated by the acting out of its main events as a play. Such plays are called 'passion-plays'. The word 'passion' has changed its meaning; it used to mean 'suffering'. A passion-play is a play about the sufferings of Jesus of Nazareth.

One of the most famous passion-plays is that performed every ten years by the villagers of Oberammergau in Bavaria, Southern Germany. It was first performed in 1634, the year after the Black Death had spread across Europe killing millions of people. The villagers of Oberammergau decided to perform the play as a sign of gratitude for being spared. Today, 350 years later, it attracts very large audiences from all over the world.

The Oberammergau play lasts for eight hours. It begins with the entry of Jesus into Jerusalem and goes on to show how

A scene from the Oberammergau Passion Play – Christ's entry in Jerusalem.

he cast the moneylenders out of the temple and clashed with the priests and other important people. This is followed by the betrayal of Jesus by Judas after the Last Supper. In the Oberammergau play there is a long interval at this point. The second half tells the story of the trials of Jesus, his crucifixion and resurrection.

When the villagers of Oberammergau made their promise in 1633 to devote a spring and a summer to performing this play they were not doing anything very original. Passion-plays were quite common. They might be performed at any time but they were all based on what happened, and still happens, in Christian churches during the week we call Holy Week.

The first Holy Week – a real drama

The reason that Christians have always celebrated the events of Holy Week through acting them out again and again is because the first Holy Week was itself a real drama. Lots of things were done. Not very much was said.

Christians do not perform these plays simply to remember the events which went on in Jerusalem nearly two thousand years ago. They do it because they want to try and recapture what those days felt like and to sense what was really happening.

Religion is often concerned with trying to express what words alone will not say. When Jesus rode into Jerusalem his actions spoke louder than words. Although they sometimes try very hard, Christians cannot say exactly what the suffering and death of Jesus means to them. In the same way, Jesus could not explain to his disciples exactly why he had to suffer and die.

Perhaps this is why we have festivals. With actions, music, singing, playing and dancing we can say more than words can ever tell. This seems to be particularly true of Holy Week. From the very earliest times Christians have always celebrated the Thursday and Friday. Later they made Palm Sunday a special day, too. Finally, they began to use the whole week. However, Palm Sunday, Maundy Thursday and Good Friday continue to be much more important than the other days.

The Saturday of Holy Week seems to be a day on which little happens. In a sense this is true, but it is still important. We have said that Holy Week is like a play. It would be more accurate to say that it is like the first part of a two-act play. In the play acted out at Oberammergau the interval is set to come after the events of Maundy Thursday. The break in the drama of Holy Week, however, comes after Good Friday: Saturday is an 'interval' which lasts all day.

The second act in the drama of Holy Week is called *Easter*. As soon as you finish the Holy Week section of this book you should go straight on to the Easter section. The two belong together. Holy Week and Easter are like night and day. If you stop at Good Friday you will miss the sunrise.

2

Palm Sunday

The first day of Holy Week is a Sunday, known as Palm Sunday. The way in which it is celebrated has changed very little over hundreds of years.

In the year A.D. 390 a Spanish nun called Etheria (or Egeria) went to Jerusalem on a pilgrimage. She wrote down what happened while she was there. On the Sunday before Easter the normal service of worship did not begin in a building. It started outside one of the gates of the city. The congregation stood while a verse was read from the Gospel, Matthew 21:9. Then, holding branches of palm trees or olive trees above their heads, the people followed the bishop through the gate and into the city, singing as they went.

Many things have changed in the world since that time but if Etheria was to come back today on a Palm Sunday morning she would know exactly what was happening. This would be particularly true if she came back to Spain, Italy or Greece. There, on Palm Sunday morning she would be likely to see processions through the streets similar to the one she joined walking through old Jerusalem.

In Britain a full procession is less likely to be seen in the streets but in some churches processions are held. Many services on that day start outside the building. A part of the story is read aloud (often the exact piece which Etheria heard) and then the congregation, singing a hymn and carrying

Christ riding on an ass. This type of 'Palmesel' was carried in procession on Palm Sunday in many towns in Europe. This one comes from Germany and was made in the fifteenth century.

branches, sometimes of willow rather than palm, follow the priest or minister into the church.

During the service which follows small crosses made of palm leaves will be given out and the full story of the first Palm Sunday will be told.

The story of Palm Sunday

The Jewish day of rest (Shabbat) falls on a Saturday. Therefore, Sunday morning to Jews is what Monday morning is to Christians – the first day of the working week.

Jesus had spent the previous day, the Jewish Sabbath (Shabbat), at the house of some friends at Bethany, a small village only a few kilometres from Jerusalem. It was nearly Passover time and Jesus was joining all the pilgrims who were visiting Jerusalem for this most important of Jewish festivals.

His followers, or disciples, were nervous. Jesus had been travelling around Judaea preaching for about three years. He had made many friends but he had also made some very powerful enemies, nearly all of whom lived in Jerusalem. Now Jesus had come to the Holy City itself and was about to enter it. How he made his entrance was very important because it would state clearly what he was claiming to be.

For centuries the Jews had believed that one day a Messiah would come. This Messiah would be a great leader come to make his followers God's people on earth. The Jews were under the rule of the Romans, who were always on the look-out for anyone who might be the sort of leader to start a rebellion. Many of the Jews hoped Jesus would do just that. They wanted to see a leader like a general, going into battle; such a leader as might appear mounted on a beautiful horse.

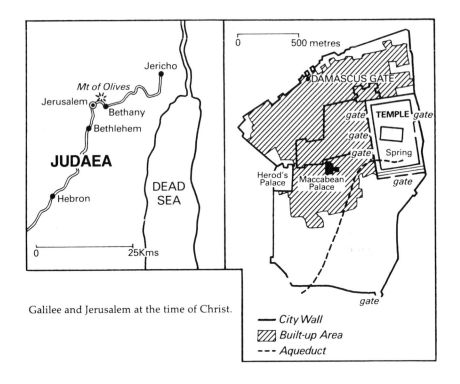

City Wall

Built-up Area

Aqueduct

Jesus sent two of his disciples to find a donkey which he had secretly arranged to borrow beforehand. On this lowly animal he rode towards the city, his disciples walking behind. When they saw him coming, some of the crowd pulled branches from nearby palms and olive trees. These they waved, putting some on the ground for the donkey to walk on. They cheered and started to call out, 'Hosanna! [Save us, we pray!] God bless the one who is coming in His name.'

A simple journey thus became a procession. Followed by the crowd, Jesus made his way through the narrow streets of the city to the great temple. He stopped and looked around at what was going on in the temple courtyard. Then he turned and went out through the gate and back to the village of Bethany.

Read the story as it is written in the Gospels. The shortest version is in Mark 11:1–11. Notice that there is no mention of Jesus saying anything at all during the whole incident.

Holy Week

Perhaps he was chatting or greeting people but he appears to have made no speeches, nor to have said anything about what he was doing.

Meanings of Palm Sunday

The story of Palm Sunday is in three parts. First of all there was the incident with the donkey. Donkeys were, and still are in some countries, beasts of burden. A king or a general would never be seen on a donkey. He would want to show how powerful he was. To do that he would ride on the best horse available. Surely if Jesus wanted to demonstrate that he was the Messiah (the Christ) he would also choose a horse. Jesus had other ideas about what the Messiah would be like. He had tried to teach his followers that the Messiah would be a suffering servant. Some of them could not understand him. They preferred to think of a military leader. But Jesus knew the Jewish scriptures and so did many of the crowd. In one of the books of a lesser known prophet, Zechariah, there was a clear statement:

Behold your King will come to you very humbly riding on an ass.
(Zechariah 9:9)

Secondly, there was the procession through the gate of the Holy City of Jerusalem. Until fairly modern times it has been a custom for a triumphant king or general to ride or walk in procession through a gateway or an arch. Sometimes arches were built at enormous expense for just this purpose, not only in ancient Rome but more recently in places like Paris (The Arc de Triomphe) and London (Marble Arch and Admiralty Arch).

Of course, many people travelled in and out of the gates of Jerusalem on donkeys, just as today many thousands of people daily drive under Admiralty Arch in London. It was the actions of the people which changed what might have been an ordinary journey into a triumphal procession. Leaders today are given what we call 'the red-carpet treatment'. The red carpet, rolled out to a car or to an aeroplane, is a symbol of greatness. The crowd on this particular Sunday tore branches

Remains of a Roman triumphal arch. This one spans the biblical 'street called Straight' in Damascus.

from nearby palm trees and used those as a 'carpet' for the same purpose. Jesus had become known and loved for his teaching and healing. We are left to guess that it was largely the country people, who were in Jerusalem for Passover, who led the cheering, rather than the city dwellers of the capital. To ordinary bystanders, both Jewish and Roman, Jesus may have appeared to be just a man coming into Jerusalem on a donkey.

Holy Week

So what? Why all the fuss? To those who saw it as a deeply symbolic action, however, it was a very important moment. Jerusalem was not only the capital city. It was, for them, the spiritual centre of the world. Here was a king coming to inherit his kingdom in triumph. Here was a true religion about to conquer the false religion going on all around.

The third part of the story comes right at the end. Once in the city, Jesus went to the temple. This was the very centre of the Jewish religion. It was as if God Himself lived there. Jesus looked around at all that was going on, then turned and left. Next morning he would be back.

The drama of Palm Sunday is to be found in a king coming into his kingdom. Some people are glad; others are resentful. The resentful people are those already in charge. If the true king is to inherit his kingdom he will have to assert his authority. He must overcome the evil which is all around him but he knows, better than his supporters, that the evil might destroy him. The king might die. In the middle of the triumph there is also great danger.

Later on in the week Jesus himself was to put all these feelings into a story. Read it now. It is in Luke's Gospel 20:9–18.

The following hymn is perhaps the most common sung on Palm Sunday. It too expresses the same mood. Read it carefully. Look up in the dictionary any words you do not understand.

Ride on! ride on in majesty!
Hark! all the tribes 'Hosanna!' cry;
O Saviour meek, pursue thy road
With palms and scattered garments strowed.

Ride on! ride on in majesty!
In lowly pomp ride on to die;
O Christ, thy triumphs now begin
O'er captive death and conquered sin.

Ride on! ride on in majesty!
The wingèd squadrons of the sky
Look down with sad and wondering eyes
To see the approaching sacrifice.

Ride on! ride on in majesty!
Thy last and fiercest strife is nigh;
The Father on his sapphire throne
Awaits his own annointed Son.

Ride on! ride on in majesty!
In lowly pomp ride on to die;
Bow thy meek head to mortal pain,
Then take, O God, thy power and reign.

More about what happens today

It is easy to see how Palm Sunday got its name from the palm branches used in the procession. In most of northern Europe palm trees do not grow and, for centuries, willow branches were used instead. The willow tree – and particularly the type we call pussy willow – is among the first trees to put out buds, the first sure sign of spring.

Not surprisingly, there is a great deal of pre-Christian or nature worship connected with the willow. We find in many places that the willows used in Palm Sunday services are used for other purposes as well.

In the Black Forest region of Germany tall poles are decorated with pussy willow and colourful streamers. They are carried in procession to church to be blessed and then put out in the fields. It was once believed that this would ensure good crops. In Austria, too, farmers and their families walk through the fields on Palm Sunday afternoon saying prayers and leaving small branches of willow in each field and barn. In Greece, the priests bless willow branches. They are then given out to the congregation, who take them home. It is a custom for farmers to use them to sprinkle holy water on to cattle.

In eastern parts of Finland the day before Palm Sunday is

known as Willowswitch Saturday. Children get up early, cut twigs of willow and decorate them with ribbon streamers. Then they go from farm to farm beating the women lightly with their bundles of twigs (switches), chanting a rhyme wishing them good health and many children.

All of these are interesting examples of how old fertility rites continue even after centuries of Christianity. Early Christian missionaries may have thought they had converted the symbols but the old meanings are still known by many.

One of the strangest Palm Sunday celebrations goes on in parts of Hungary. It, too, was a pagan ritual that has been given a Christian meaning. No doubt different people still have different interpretations. It is the acting out of a traditional fight between Prince Cibere and King Bone.

Prince Cibere is the symbol of winter. He is made of rag and straw and is the 'baddy'. On Shrove Tuesday he fights with King Bone (the 'goody') and wins. His victory means that everyone goes hungry (the fast of Lent starts after Shrove Tuesday) until Palm Sunday, when there is another battle. This time King Bone is the victor. The watching crowd carries the effigy of Prince Cibere around the village. He is then burned or drowned, taking hunger and sorrow with him.

Palm Sunday is the focus of a battle between good and evil. In ancient religions this battle was best seen in the conflict between winter (evil) and spring (good). For Christians the battle took on a new significance and ancient customs were incorporated in their religious festivals.

3

Monday, Tuesday and Wednesday

Although there are almost no public festivities to mark the next three days of Holy Week, groups of Christians will meet in their churches. There are no processions. It is a quiet and solemn time.

In this short chapter it is possible only to outline the stories which Christians will be thinking about on these three days. The stories themselves help us to understand why the events of Thursday and Friday took place.

Monday – the cleansing of the temple

On Palm Sunday Jesus had looked at what was going on in the temple area. Then, without saying or doing anything, he walked away. Next day he came back, walked into the temple courtyard, which was being used as a street market, and pushed over some of the stalls. 'The Scriptures tell us "God's house shall be a house of prayer",' Jesus told the people gathered there. 'But you have turned it into a robbers' den.' He then told off some women who were using the temple yard as a short cut, before striding away. Read the story in Mark 11:15–19.

This is another example of the drama of Holy Week. Jesus did not make a long speech about what he thought was wrong in the temple. Nor did he lose his temper. The authorities could have dealt with these two things quite easily. By doing something, by acting in a controlled way, Jesus set the priests and the rulers a real problem. Somehow they had to respond but they had to be careful not to upset those who were sympathetic towards Jesus. Nevertheless, they began to plan how they could get rid of him.

Tuesday – the questions of Holy Week

On the Tuesday of Holy Week Jesus' enemies tried to get him to talk. They did this by trying to force him to answer very pointed questions by which they hoped to discredit him in front of the people. Each one contained a catch. Mark's Gospel tells us about four questions.

The first is the question of authority. By what authority did Jesus do things, such as upsetting the stalls in the temple? It is a catch question to try to get Jesus to claim to be the Son of God, which will not only sound boastful but could also result in him being tried for blasphemy. Read the story in Mark 11:27–33.

The second question is about loyalty. If Jesus sided with Caesar and the Romans the crowd would turn to hating him. If he openly said they should defy Rome he would be arrested. The story is told in Mark 12:13–17.

The third question is just a silly one. It was meant to sound clever so that Jesus would appear not to know as much as the religious leaders. They hoped it would also show if he was willing to take sides. The 'professors' of the day were always arguing about pointless things of this sort. You can read about it in Mark 12:18–27.

The final question is about what is important. It is a much more serious question and Jesus gives a serious reply. There were many books of Jewish law and much, much more which was not written down. Jesus is asked which is the most important bit. In reply he picks out two short passages from the Jewish scriptures. You can find them in Deuteronomy 6:5 and in Leviticus 19:18. To love God first and to love your fellow human beings matters above all else. They are God's children, is what Jesus is saying. It seemed very simple. Perhaps it was the religious leaders who had made it complicated and difficult. The story appears in Mark 12:28-34.

These four questions and all that is behind them are what Christians who keep the whole of Holy Week as a special time of prayer and reflection will think about on the Tuesday.

Wednesday – good examples and what the future holds in store

There is a story in Mark 12:41-44 which seems to sum up much of what Jesus had said and done since entering Jerusalem. At the entrance to the temple were the collecting bowls in which pilgrims put their offerings. Jesus watched. Many rich people made a great show of putting in lots of money and the priests, or at least some of them, were very pleased. Then along came a very poor widow who put in two small, copper coins, almost worthless. But it was all she had. Jesus pointed to her as the best example. The value of a gift is what it costs the giver, not how much it is worth to other people. It is what people *are*, not what they *say* or even seem to do, that is important. But that was not how the religious leaders saw it. Jesus was saying that they were hypocrites and that the poor and weak were important, not them. They hated him for that.

4

Maundy Thursday

In Britain, the Thursday of Holy Week is called Maundy Thursday. The word 'Maundy' comes from the Latin word 'mandatum', which means 'commandment'. It was on the Thursday of Holy Week that Jesus was reported as saying to his disciples, 'A new commandment I give you; love one another'. In Latin this begins, 'Mandatum novum do vobis', and it has been sung as an anthem in Roman Catholic churches on this day for hundreds of years.

In other parts of the world the day has different names. It is known as Green Thursday in many parts of Germany and Czechoslovakia, and as Sheer, or 'Clean' Thursday in some other countries.

Both of these names arose out of an old practice. On this Thursday many people used to finish a period of penance which they had been observing all through Lent. They might, quite literally, have been wearing sackcloth and ashes. On Clean Thursday they would clean themselves up and cut their hair and beards. It was also the day on which church altars were ceremonially washed. Probably the habit of spring cleaning is a present-day connection with this custom. On Green Thursday in Germany and Czechoslovakia there was the ritual of giving a green branch to all who had finished their penance. Today the tradition remains in the custom of eating green salad on this day.

No doubt the greenery also reveals customs which go back

long before the coming of Christianity, such as we have seen with the willow branches. In Finland this is very obvious. In rural areas the name Kiira Thursday is sometimes still used. The Kiira were evil spirits which had to be driven away from the farms. Even today children sometimes run around the farmyards with cowbells tied to their necks – an old-fashioned way of scaring away the spirits.

A more widespread custom is the preparation of Easter eggs on this day, often richly decorated (see the book *Easter* in this series).

Among all the customs belonging to Maundy Thursday two things stand out. In the first place it is a day of humility as shown by the penitents. Secondly, it is remembered as the day when the main act of worship in Christianity was begun. This we know by various names, such as the Mass, the Eucharist, Holy Communion or the Lord's Supper.

The act of humility
In John's Gospel we read that Jesus took water and a towel and washed the feet of his disciples (John 13:4-5). In the hot, dusty land of Palestine it was the task of the lowest servant to wash the feet of the master of the house and any guests. Here is another piece of drama: Jesus, the master, washes the feet of his followers.

The Christian Church has followed this example for many centuries. In early times monks washed one another's feet on this day. Then it became the custom to call beggars to the monastery to have their feet washed and be given money. In many churches today, the priest continues the custom by washing the feet of some of his parishioners.

In Rome the Pope washes the feet of twelve men, representing Jesus' twelve disciples. At one time the custom spread to the kings and queens of Europe. In Austria, for example, the emperor used to do this for twelve old men and then give them a lavish dinner.

A similar ceremony was once performed by the monarch in Britain, but King James II was the last to carry out this traditional act of humility. After him the task was given to the King's Almoner but even that stopped in 1754. The ceremony was continued in the giving of money to the poor. Today this is carried on in the annual Maundy service. During the Queen's reign the Maundy service has been held in churches all over the country, including York Minster, Tewkesbury Abbey and Winchester Cathedral, and several times at Westminster Abbey. In 1986 the service was held at Chichester Cathedral.

The Maundy service
The Lord High Almoner attends the Queen as she walks in procession between two rows of the Yeomen of the Guard. The Queen and other dignitaries carry small bouquets of sweet-smelling flowers, reminding us of the bunches of herbs once carried by the nobility as a precaution against disease when mixing with the poor (a pocket full of posies!).

A Yeoman of the Guard carries the purses of Maundy money on a gold tray. Each old person chosen to receive the money is given two purses, a white one containing the special Maundy money, and a red one containing ordinary coins. Food and clothes were once given out but this custom was discontinued.

H.M. the Queen presents Maundy money at Exeter Cathedral. Note the long strings attached to each purse.

The purses are given to a number of people according to the monarch's age. Thus in 1983 the Queen gave fifty-seven men and fifty-seven women fifty-seven coins each. The total value of the coins in each red purse has now been fixed at five pounds. The coins in the white purse are exact replicas of those used in the days of King Charles I and include penny, twopenny, threepenny and fourpenny pieces.

The coins are sought after by collectors willing to pay a high price for them but those people chosen to receive them hardly ever part with them.

Maundy money. The largest coin is about the same size as a new penny.

The Last Supper

When Jesus had finished the task of washing feet he and his disciples carried on with their meal. What he did and said that night has remained as the central act of worship in Christian churches, commemorated in the Lord's Supper.

Read the story in Mark 14:17–25. Imagine the scene. The men sat, or rather lounged, on couches or benches around a table. A large dish containing a meat stew, in this case lamb, stood in the middle of the table. Each person was given a hunk of bread, broken from a loaf, to dip into the common dish.

On this occasion as Jesus broke the bread he said something very surprising. 'This is my body,' he told the twelve as he passed the pieces round. Then he poured out the wine saying, 'This is my blood'. The disciples all ate and drank. The meal

Holy Week

ended and they set off in the darkness to go through the woods on the Mount of Olives back to Bethany. On the way, Jesus was surrounded and arrested. It was the last supper they ever had together.

Meanings of the Last Supper

Whole books have been written about the meaning of Jesus' action and words at the Last Supper. Christians have argued with one another for centuries about what it all means. Nevertheless it has been, and goes on being, repeated over and over again. Of all the dramatic actions of Holy Week this is the most often repeated. Roman Catholics know this act of worship as the Mass. Other Churches call it by various names such as Holy Communion, Eucharist or simply the Lord's Supper. The fact that there are so many names reflects many different ways of looking at it.

Because the early Christians used Jesus' own words and said they were eating his body and drinking his blood they were sometimes accused of being like cannibals. But they could not find a better way of saying what they felt than by simply repeating his words and actions. When we eat food and take drink it becomes part of us. It helps us grow and keeps us alive. After Jesus had finally left them, his followers felt that they were close to him still. St Paul talked of the great mystery of being *in* Christ and having Christ *in* him.

For many Christians it is not possible to explain in words at all, so week by week and on special festivals they simply go to church to hear again the words 'This is my body' and 'This is my blood' and to receive the bread and the wine.

The Last Supper of Jesus and his disciples is a deeply symbolic event, acted out thousands of times every day in different parts of the world wherever Christians meet.

5

Good Friday
and Beyond

Good Friday is the day when Christians everywhere remember the death of Jesus on a cross (the crucifixion) and his burial. In some parts of Europe the day is known as Black Friday, which might seem a better description. The word 'Good', however, was probably once 'God's'. The change has taken place in many expressions, like 'Good Heavens' for 'God's Heaven', and 'Goodbye' for 'God be with you'.

Ceremonies and traditions all over the world reflect the solemnity and sadness of the first Good Friday. On that day Jesus was tried in front of the Roman Governor, Pontius Pilate, and King Herod. Mocked as a king, he was given a cloak to wear and a crown of thorns, and condemned to death. Then he was nailed to a cross and left there to die.

Read the story for yourselves in any of the Gospels. It can be found in the following chapters: Mark:15; Luke:23; Matthew:27 or John:19.

The Jews of the time worked out their hours from dawn, which came at around six o'clock. So the 'third hour' mentioned in the Gospels comes at nine o'clock in the morning, while the 'ninth hour' is about three o'clock in the afternoon.

Many churches observe all six hours of the crucifixion with reading, prayers and long periods of silence. People come and go during this time. There are also processions and, in particular, the regular procession inside Roman Catholic churches to the Stations of the Cross.

A 'station' describes a stopping point. On Good Friday morning, led by the priest, the congregation walk around the church stopping in front of each of fourteen pictures or carvings on the walls. In some modern Roman Catholic churches a fifteenth picture has been added.

Some of the incidents these pictures describe we have already dealt with but there are others we have not mentioned. Most of them can be looked up in the Gospels. A few belong to tradition.

The church in which such a procession takes place will probably be bare. Ornaments will have been removed; there may be black drapings over the altar. Sometimes a hooded cross is carried at the front of the procession. This is a cross covered over with a black cloth.

In recent years other churches have restarted the idea of Good Friday processions. Their Stations of the Cross are rather different. For example, in the city of Exeter members of all the central churches meet together outside the offices of the city council. This is the first station. Here they gather on the pavement, listen to the reading of the first part of the Passion story, say a short prayer and move on through the city. The other stations are such places as a central bank, the shopping centre, a large hotel, a busy crossroads and so on – all the major points of life in a modern city. Finally they process into one of their churches for a short service. They are led all the way by a large, bare wooden cross, held high.

Today this sort of activity is becoming more and more common. In many other countries the customs have never died out. In Greece, after a long period in church, remembering the six hours on the cross, the body is taken from the crucifix and the empty cross is paraded around the town. In the villages of Crete a funeral pall is carried ceremoniously around the streets at dusk. These processions often end with a bonfire on which an effigy of Judas Iscariot, who betrayed Jesus, is burnt. In Italy, Spain and other European countries it is a day of

A Good Friday procession in Perpignan, France. This picture contains many of the symbols connected with Holy Week. The bearers of the 'coffin' are dressed in red and black, above the crucifix red flowers are held, and in the background are palms. The coffin too is draped in black.

symbols such as coffins, crowns of thorns, nails, whips and thirty pieces of silver.

Good Friday is a fast day. For some this may mean not eating any food at all but for most it means that certain foods are avoided. Traditionally, meat is not eaten at all on Good Friday; fish is the main dish instead. In past times fish was commonly a substitute for meat on every Friday of the year. It remains a fairly strong tradition on Good Friday.

Hot cross buns

The most popular food connected with Good Friday is the hot cross bun. It has a very long history. The Greeks and Romans made small wheat cakes marked with a cross at the spring festivals. The round bun, it is thought, represented the full moon with the cross being the four quarters of the moon. The Greeks offered these cakes to their gods Apollo and Astarte.

The Jews followed a custom of eating unleavened bread at the Feast of the Passover which, as we have seen, was happening at the time of the crucifixion (see *Passover* in this series).

Early Christian missionaries in northern Europe found that small wheaten cakes were made at this time of year on which crosses were inscribed. These were supposed to ward off evil. Our traditional hot cross buns no doubt come from these early customs.

It was once believed that sacred cakes like these would not go mouldy like ordinary cakes. It was a custom to hang them in the house for a year, as a charm to keep away evil spirits.

For Christians, hot cross buns were reminders of the crucifixion. Over the years such buns became a food only for Good Friday morning, eaten hot and made with spices as a reminder of the spices in the Good Friday story of Luke 23:56 and John 19:39.

Other Good Friday customs

In some places Good Friday is known as 'Long Rope Day'. Families in Sussex coast villages used mooring ropes of fishing boats to skip with on the beaches. It was believed this would bring good catches in coming months. Also in Sussex the game of marbles has traditionally been played on Good Friday. It is thought this may be connected with the crucifixion story of soldiers who cast lots and played dice at the foot of the cross (see John 19:24). Today, at Tinsley Green in Sussex, the annual British Marble Championship is held.

The sepulchre

Whatever may happen outside, the main activity of Good Friday goes on inside churches. In some, as the day comes to an end and darkness falls, there is a small, dramatic acting out of the burial of Jesus. A crucifix (a cross bearing an image of Jesus) and the host (the bread which has been consecrated for the Eucharist) are 'buried' in a special sepulchre in the church. Easter sepulchres are usually made of wood, richly carved and decorated but in many churches, and especially old ones, a permanent sepulchre was built into the stone wall of the chancel.

As the 'body of Christ' is buried in the sepulchre, candles are lit. It seems to be the end of the story but it is not. There is more, much more, to come.

Holy Saturday – Easter Eve

The last day of Holy Week is a day of waiting and preparation. It is the day after a funeral when all the activity seems to be over but when there is a feeling of emptiness everywhere. Holy Week began with a mixture of triumph and tension. The worst seems to have happened. The king is dead.

However, the mood begins to change. Easter Saturday is a day of transformation. Where ornaments have been taken out of a church for Good Friday they are brought back in, clean and shining. Altars which have been bare or draped in black are covered in gold or white. Flowers appear, often in large quantities. Suddenly there is colour everywhere.

In some parts of the world the change is sudden. Celebrations begin, especially at dusk, in some Mediterranean countries. Throughout Eastern Europe and Russia the change comes at midnight, when candles will be lit and the shout will be heard, 'He is risen'.

In Roman Catholic churches a vigil will be kept in front of the sepulchre. This will go on through the night until dawn. The hours of darkness are spent in the solemn mood of Holy Week but as light comes so does celebration. The tomb is empty. The 'body' is no longer there. Christ has risen. Easter has begun.

Holy Week is a long drama, rich in symbols. But it is only half the story. No one should leave the drama at this point. The second half is Easter. The two belong together as day belongs to night.

Easter

Norma Fairbairn and Jack Priestley

Contents

Russian Christians celebrate Easter

Easter

Introduction

Easter is all about new life. It comes at a time when spring is in the air. It is a festival about hope for the future. There is nothing sad about Easter. All that is in the past. Winter has gone. The dark days are over; there are signs of new life everywhere.

For one group of people it is a festival above all other festivals. Every Sunday of the year Christians remember the Resurrection — the coming back to life of Jesus Christ. Easter day, for Christians, is like all the Sundays of the year rolled into one. It comes two days after Good Friday, when Jesus was crucified, but Good Friday and Easter are as far apart as darkness and light. For Christians, Easter is when sadness is suddenly turned into happiness, when despair turns into joy, when that which seemed dead is suddenly alive again, and is alive for evermore. Easter is a festival about the future, about believing in tomorrow.

On Easter day Christian churches all over the world are full of colour and flowers. The services are full of joyful singing. Everywhere there are symbols of light and laughter. The words heard most frequently are 'Christ is risen, Alleluia!'.

1

Easter Celebrations

Easter really begins at 6 p.m. on the Saturday. That is the day known as Easter Eve. It was at that time that the Jewish Sabbath came to an end, and we shall see in the next chapter why that was important for Easter.

The Saturday makes a complete break between Good Friday and Easter day. They are two quite different occasions and should not be mixed up. Not long ago it was customary for banks, shops, offices and factories to close on the Friday, open again for work on Saturday morning and then close again until Tuesday. Nowadays for many people it has become one continuous holiday but this book is only about Easter. (There is another book in this series which deals with the events of the week up to Good Friday.)

Easter is celebrated in many different ways all over the world. The celebrations are a mixture of religious services and all sorts of other activities, some of them quite crazy although we can give only a very few examples here. There are many more which it would be fun to find out about, especially the ones which happen near where you live.

There are three days of Easter festivities, Easter Eve, Easter day and Easter Monday, and we can divide the celebrations up like that, although some of them go on for more than one day. There are things that happen on Easter Tuesday as well, like the two-hundred-year-old custom of giving out large buns known as 'twopenny starvers' to the choir boys of St Michael's Church, Bristol.

Easter Eve

In many parts of the world Easter Eve is a day of getting ready. It is a day of cooking and washing and decorating. A lot goes on unnoticed and, particularly, inside churches there is a rush of activity. On Good Friday at the end of forty days of Lent, the churches are dark and depressing. They are often draped in black and purple and all the ornaments have been removed or covered. On Easter Eve it is all transformed; silver and gold colours appear everywhere — on the altar; the Bible markers; the pulpit cloth; and the priests' clothes, or vestments. The ornaments are brought back and masses of spring flowers decorate every corner.

In some homes, too, a great deal of work goes on, often in the kitchen. Special foods are got ready. It is traditional to eat roast lamb on Easter day but in many parts of the world it is accompanied by all sorts of other foods which also have to be prepared.

It is getting the Easter eggs ready which is the most common custom in many homes on Easter Eve. But in some parts of the world this is an operation which has already been going on for weeks. In Eastern Europe, in particular, decorating eggs is a work of art. The most detailed patterns are worked on to them, often with paint but sometimes with wax and dye.

In Poland Easter eggs, called *pisanki,* are real hens' eggs which have been 'blown' by piercing them with a needle at each end and then carefully blowing out the contents. A wax pattern is then made with the needle. The eggshell is dipped in dye which colours all the surface except where there is wax. This can be repeated with different colours, and in this way fine patterns are built up. By Easter Eve the finishing touches are being made and, with a coat of varnish added, they are ready to give away next morning. Some of these eggs last for years and years and have become family heirlooms.

The same sort of loving care goes into decorating eggs in other countries such as Hungary and Czechoslovakia. Sometimes messages in very small writing, or passages from the Bible are etched into the pattern.

In Lithuania there is a tradition of making 'look inside' eggs which takes an equally long time. Just like our chocolate eggs these artificial eggs are large and hollow but they are all in one piece with a small hole at each end. Inside, modelled in fondant, is a whole landscape with tiny trees and bushes, hills, rabbits and chickens.

Decorated Easter eggs

Easter

These are preparations for Easter day. But just occasionally the Easter celebrations themselves begin on Easter Eve. This is especially true in Sicily, for example, where traditionally the Resurrection has always been celebrated on the Saturday. The Sicilians say that as they are nearer to Palestine than the rest of Italy they heard about the Resurrection a day earlier than anyone else. Other Italians say that the trouble with the Sicilians is that they are always so fond of merrymaking that they just can't put up with the seriousness of Lent and the sorrow of Good Friday for a moment longer.

In Britain too there are some places where Easter begins early. At Barrow in Furness there is an old tradition that the Furness Morris Men perform an old mummers' play on Easter Saturday and Easter Monday. The play itself tells of a battle between St George and a host of odd characters with names like Bold Hector, the King of Egypt, Tosspot and the Bold Slasher.

Bacup Nutters Dance

Easter 81

At Bacup, in Lancashire, Easter Saturday is the occasion for the performance of the Nutters' Dance. Eight men with blackened faces, wearing white caps, black breeches, red and white shirts, white stockings and decorated wooden clogs, dance through the town. As they go they clap the 'nuts', which are the wooden discs from the tops of cotton bobbins used in weaving. These they attach to their waists, hands and knees.

It is hard to say just how or why some of these customs began. Some of them are more a celebration of spring than of the Christian Resurrection and show that the old ways of two thousand years ago have never really died out.

Easter day

In parts of northern Europe Easter day begins at nightfall on Saturday with bonfires, around which there is singing and dancing. In the Hartz Mountains of Germany giant wooden wheels with straw tied to the spokes are set alight and rolled down the slopes. The fields where they come to rest are considered to be lucky and the farmer who owns them will have good crops. This is still a spring festival but as the night passes the festival becomes more and more a Christian celebration.

The first Easter story tells how Mary Magdalene set out 'before it was yet light', and this is remembered in many parts of the world. In some parts of Africa it is customary for young women, dressed in white, to go round the houses singing Easter hymns so that people awake to the good news that Christ is risen.

In parts of America many people spend the whole night together waiting for the sunrise. America is a huge continent and it is daylight in the east five hours before the sun rises on the West coast. The first to greet the sun on Easter morning are the people who gather on Cadillac Mountain in Maine. At the town of Lawton in Oklahoma thousands of worshippers watch a six-hour night-time pageant about the life of Jesus. It ends with the Resurrection scene just as dawn breaks over the mountain top. Many similar services are held across the U.S.A. including one in the famous Hollywood Bowl.

Hollywood Bowl

These American practices are a revival of a tradition that has been going on in the Church in Greece and Russia for nearly two thousand years. For the Eastern Orthodox Church there is no festival like Easter. The service begins on the stroke of midnight. The church is in total darkness as a priest comes out from a door in the sanctuary at the front. He holds a single lighted candle, the only light in the building. His voice breaks the silence. 'Come, ye,' he calls. 'Come and partake of the never-setting light and glorify Christ, who is risen from the dead.'

The members of the congregation come forward one by one. Each holds a candle which is lit from the priest's candle and then passed on to a neighbour, until the whole church is ablaze with flickering light. The priest leads the way out of the church. Once outside he reads the Easter story from the Gospel. As he finishes he chants, 'Christos anesti' (Christ is risen). The congregation take up the chant and reply, 'He is risen indeed.' In some communist countries where attempts have been made to do away with Christianity this ceremony in the street, even in the middle of Moscow, has become a yearly act of witness. Many have been put in prison for doing it.

In England midnight services are not very common at Easter (although see Chapter 3 on Easter vigil). They are more associated with Christmas. Often the first indication of Easter day is the noise of bells from church towers. Traditionally they were kept silent throughout Lent, though this is not done today. On Good Friday a single, muffled bell is sometimes tolled as at a funeral. But on Easter morning they ring out in peal after peal with all the energy that the bellringers can muster.

Easter is a morning festival. It is usually at breakfast that the presents of Easter eggs and other things are given and it is in the morning that the main church services are held. Often there are more people in church that morning than at any other time of the year. It is customary too in some churches for the Easter offering to be given to the priest, the only time of the year that this happens.

The afternoon of Easter day is traditionally taken up with outdoor activities of a type when people meet together. The springtime side of Easter comes to the fore again. It is as if this day marks the end of being shut up indoors. Life out of doors, which will go on through the summer, begins again. It is often a time for new clothes to mark the change of seasons but the custom also goes back to the religious habits of the past when people often deliberately wore old clothes during Lent or even covered themselves and their garments in ashes (see the section on Ash Wednesday, page 44).

Easter Sunday afternoon is the time of the Easter parade, the showing off of the Easter bonnets. Perhaps the best known parade nowadays is the one held in Battersea Park, London. In

Victorian times most parades were just made up of people strolling up and down the roads but the Battersea Park parade is a real festival procession with decorated floats and bands.

Easter Parade, Battersea Park

Easter Monday

Easter Sunday has a serious side to it. On the following day, Easter Monday, very little is taken seriously. It is here that we see the two sides of celebrating spring and celebrating the Resurrection coming together in one great day of fun and festivity. In Britain in particular it has been a holiday for hundreds of years — a day of fairs and races, hunting and sports meetings, open-air dancing and processions. There is probably more variety than on any other holiday. There are hundreds of different local traditions. Unfortunately, there is room here to deal with only one of the more unusual Easter Monday celebrations, Hare Pie Scramble and Bottle Kicking at Hallaton in Leicestershire.

The story which is told to explain the custom is that many centuries ago a local lady crossing a field was chased by a bull.

Easter

Hallaton Hare Pie. The bottles can be seen in the background

Easter

She was only saved from being gored to death when a hare ran across the path of the bull causing it to hesitate. In gratitude the woman gave some land to the church on condition that the rector of the parish should distribute two hare pies to the parishioners every year. Making hare pie seems a strange way of showing gratitude to hares, but as we shall see in a later chapter, hares have been associated with Easter for many centuries and there is probably much more behind this particular event than this simple story suggests.

Nowadays small pieces of pie are thrown to the crowd which gathers on a mound known as Hare Pie Bank, just outside the village. There is a scramble to get a portion of the pie and the ceremony is accompanied by much eating and drinking.

The 'bottles' which are kicked are not bottles at all but beer barrels. There are three barrels — two full and one empty. One of the full barrels is placed on top of the mound. The men of Hallaton and the next village of Medbourne face one another. At a given signal each team tries to get the barrel back to its own village. The winners drink the beer. Then they start again but to make it easier the second time round, the empty barrel is used, although the winners take possession of the third barrel, which is full!

Are there any similar local customs near where you live, or were there in the past? What have any such customs got to do with the Easter story?

2

Stories at Easter

For Christians the Easter stories are the stories of how Jesus rose from the dead and showed himself to his followers.

But the word 'Easter' is not a Christian word at all. It comes from the name of a pagan goddess Eostre or Eastre. Her name meant 'the dawn' so that her festival, which took place every spring, was also about light and waking up to new life.

It was probably the great Christian Saint Bede (A.D. 673–735) from Jarrow in the north-east of England who first joined the two festivals together. It was one way of converting the pagans to Christianity. The name 'Easter' was kept but it was the risen Christ who was worshipped. As we see, however, old customs die hard and some of the symbols of our modern Easter probably come from Eostre's festival even if they have long since been given Christian meanings.

The Christian stories of the Resurrection are told over and over again at Easter. They are to be found at the end of the four Gospels. The Gospels of Luke and John tell the stories in much more detail than the other two. You should read these stories as they are told in the Bible. They appear in the following Gospels: Matthew 28; Mark 16; Luke 24; and John 20, 21.

There are six different stories although one of them is really about the Ascension, when Jesus finally left his followers. Here we shall only look at the other five. There are differences in the way of the Gospel writers relate the happenings and it must be said that there is something mysterious about the stories they tell. We should remember that the disciples could not fully understand events themselves. They were dazed and bewildered. In putting these stories down they were telling of what went on inside their heads as much as what was happening outside.

One thing does seem certain. At the beginning of these incidents all the disciples were convinced that Jesus was dead. At the end the same disciples were quite sure that he was alive and that they had seen him — even though at first they had refused to believe it. We know that many of them spent the rest of their lives convincing others. If they had not done so there would be no Christian Church today.

Let us look at the five stories separately:

The appearance of Jesus to Mary (and other women):
(Matthew 28: 1—10; Mark 16: 1—8; Luke 24: 1—12; John 20; 1—18)

All the Gospel writers agree that the first appearance of Jesus was at dawn on the Sunday morning to a woman, or women, near the tomb. John says that Mary Magdalene was on her own, Luke says she had two others with her. Matthew and Mark say she had only one companion but one says it was Salome and the other says it was a woman called Mary.

There are differences too in how the message was given, whether by one angel, or by two, or by Jesus himself.

But notice also the things that are the same. No one could go to the tomb on the Saturday because it was the Sabbath until dusk. The tradition that it was at first light on the Sunday morning is very strong. So are the details that the stone was already rolled away, that it was the women who were first on the scene, and that the majority of the men refused to believe the story.

The appearance on the Emmaus road:
(Mark 16: 12—13; Luke 24: 13—34)

Only two of the four Gospel writers tell this story and only the account by Luke has any detail. It is about two of the men who refused to believe what had happened to the women at the tomb and to whom Jesus appeared as they travelled to Emmaus, though at first they did not recognize him. Only when they stopped to eat together did they realize it was Jesus as 'he took the bread, and blessed it, and brake, and gave to them' (Compare this story with the one in Luke 22: 19.)

Though darkness had fallen the two men hurried back the twenty kilometres to Jerusalem. The other disciples had locked themselves in and the two had some difficulty in getting them to open the door. Even when they entered they found it hard to explain what had happened. They were as certain as the women that Jesus was alive but were unable to convince their friends.

The appearance in the upper room:
(Mark 16: 14—15.; Luke 24: 36—49; John 20: 19—25)

The two men from Emmaus were still trying to convince their friends that they had seen Jesus when suddenly, there he was in the room, though the door was shut and barred. Jesus showed them the wounds in his hands, feet and side. He spoke the Jewish greeting 'Shalom' (Peace be with you) and asked for something to eat. Frightened and puzzled the disciples offered Jesus some cooked fish. And then, as suddenly as he had come, he was gone again. After this experience all the disciples except one believed that Jesus was alive. The exception was Thomas. He was not with the other disciples at the time Jesus appeared and he refused to believe the story until he had some proof.

The appearance to doubting Thomas:
(John 20: 26—31)

It was eight days later that Jesus appeared again. This time Thomas was there and the story tells how Jesus allowed himself to be touched so that Thomas could have the proof he wanted. He also warned him that not everyone can have proof like this and then he disappeared again. Now all the close followers of Jesus believed that he had risen from the dead.

Easter

The appearance at Galilee:
(John 21: 1—25)

Only John's Gospel tells of a final appearance to the disciples who had gone back to Galilee to take up their work as fishermen again. In many details it is just like the story of the first time that Jesus called on these disciples to follow him. (read Luke 5: 2—11).

It is as if the whole story was to begin all over again and in a way this is just what happened. These fishermen did give up their jobs and their homes and they did spend the rest of their lives preaching about the risen Jesus. That is how the Christian Church began to spread, and has continued to grow down to the present day.

Just how much detail in these stories went on in the heads of the disciples and just how much happened exactly as the stories say, we shall never know. These stories are like poems. For Christians they tell the great, central truth of their faith — Christ is risen. The Resurrection came on a Sunday, which is why, right from the start, the disciples changed their sabbath day from the Jewish Saturday in order to celebrate it. The first disciples did not find the Resurrection easy to believe at first either. They could never fully explain it. All they could do was to celebrate it.

This has been the experience of countless men and women over centuries. They have, like the disciples, become convinced that Christ is risen and they have tried to express their feelings in music and poetry and paintings. They express it in festival too — in the great annual festival of Easter, when these stories are told again and again.

3

Symbols of Easter

When Saint Bede converted the festival of Eostre into the festival of Christ's Resurrection many of the old symbols became converted as well. It is perfectly true to say that many of the symbols of Easter are pagan but Christians see in them meanings belonging to their own Resurrection stories. Let us look at a few examples.

Laurel   Laurel is an evergreen shrub with a very interesting history. For centuries people have thought of it as an emblem of leadership and victory. The Greeks gave a wreath of laurel to victorious athletes and in the days of the Roman Empire army leaders who have been successful in battle had garlands of laurel placed on their heads.

Nowadays laurel is sometimes used to decorate churches at Easter time. As an evergreen it shows that life goes on through the cold darkness of winter. But the old association is also there. It is a symbol of Christ the victor who has conquered death.

Eggs   The making of chocolate eggs is a new custom, but for thousands of years, even before the time of Jesus, people have given eggs to one another as gifts in the spring. They are a sign of new life which is just about to break out. For Christians they quickly came to have a special meaning. Eggs look dead but they contain life. The shell has the shape of a cave-like tomb in which Jesus was buried. On Easter morning the rolling away of the stone was like the breaking of an egg.

In the Middle Ages it was the custom not to eat eggs during Lent. The custom of boiled eggs for breakfast on Easter morning still goes on. For a long time it was literally a breaking of the fast.

The Chick It is not difficult to see why the chick has also become a symbol of Easter. It is the chick which breaks out of the shell as Jesus broke out of the tomb. From the egg comes new life. The Easter chick is small, yellow and fluffy but it quickly grows into the large, brown hen which will lay the eggs from which other chicks will come. And so the cycle of life goes on giving rise to the old question 'Which came first, the chicken or the egg?'.

The Easter bunny In some countries it is said that the Easter bunny brings Easter eggs and children make nests for it in the garden. However, the use of young rabbits as a symbol for Easter today is probably based on a mistake. As we have already seen in the story of the Easter celebrations at Hallaton, it was the hare which was associated with Easter. Almost certainly the hare was used as a sacrifice to Eostre.

As well as these symbols there are others which are probably entirely Christian in their origins and which you will find in many churches at Easter time:

The paschal candle At Easter time in many churches there is a special, very large candle known as the paschal candle. (Paschal is simply another name for Easter. It comes from the Hebrew word *pesach,* or Passover. It was at the time of the Jewish Passover that the events of the first Christian Easter took place.) The paschal candle is large because it has to burn for forty days, from Easter until Ascension Day. Nowadays it is possible to make slow-burning candles but in the past some

A sepulchre built into a church wall

paschal candles were huge. In the Middle Ages the paschal candle in Durham Cathedral was square in shape and went up to within a man's height of the roof. The Gospels tell us that Jesus was the Light of the World. The flame of the candle is a reminder of this and it is a symbol of Jesus showing himself to the disciples during those forty days.

Easter sepulchres   An Easter sepulchre is a model of Jesus' tomb. In some old churches a permanent sepulchre was built into the wall and carved with Easter scenes.

Elsewhere they are made of wood, richly carved and decorated. They are sometimes used as part of the Easter services. In some churches the clergy act out the visit to the tomb by Mary, Peter and John to discover again that Christ has risen. In others it is the place of the Easter vigil, the waiting

An Easter garden

through the night for Easter to dawn. In every Roman Catholic church this begins at ten o'clock on the night of Easter eve.

Easter gardens A more modern custom is the making of an Easter garden to look like the garden in which Jesus' body was laid. These can often be found in schools and homes as well as churches and are made out of mosses and small spring flowers.

In the garden is a miniature sepulchre (a tomb which was either a natural cave or was cut into a hillside). By its side is a large stone, representing the stone which was rolled away to show the empty tomb. Sometimes figures of Peter, John and Mary Magdalene are placed by the tomb.

In the background there is a hill. On it stand three empty crosses, a reminder of the events of Good Friday.

These are the symbols you can see with your eyes. Each one forms only a small part of the Easter celebrations in Christian churches all over the world. There are other symbols of sound and movement. To appreciate them it is perhaps necessary to go into a church on Easter morning, to hear the singing of the Easter hymns and to see the drama of the first Easter morning acted out in many different ways.

4

The Meaning of Easter

As we have seen, it is often difficult to find the real meaning behind festivities such as Easter. The origins of certain activities are obvious while others might not be so clear. Often there may be more than one meaning, with an important message hidden within a simple story. Sometimes the stories themselves may contain different meanings.

So it is with Easter. At one level it is all about the coming of spring, rejoicing because things which seemed dead are coming to life again. At another level it is, for Christians, about the Resurrection of Christ, the conquering of death for all time.

Both are saying that life is stronger than death. While one looks at that idea in the world of nature, the other looks at it as it affects man and his place in the universe. All these ideas are brought together in the one great mixture we call a festival. Hare Pie Scramble and the Resurrection stories all go together. Perhaps we can see the two extremes in the way we fix the date of Easter and the way the New Testament talks about it.

The dating of Easter
Although we know that the events of the first Christian Easter took place at Passover time (see the book in this series *Passover*), Christians in Europe and America still celebrate the

festival according to the phases of the sun and the moon. The spring (or vernal) equinox takes place on 21 March. The word 'equinox' simply means 'equal night'. It is the day on which the sun is directly over the Equator, where there will be twelve hours of light and twelve hours of darkness. In other words the sun, which during winter has been over the southern hemisphere, is coming back to the north.

Easter day comes some time after the equinox; just when, depends on the moon. There must be one full moon after the equinox, then Easter Sunday is the first Sunday after that. This means that Easter day can be on any date between 22 March and 25 April.

. There are many people today who want Easter to be on the same date every year. Christians have no real objections because the present way of dating belongs to Eostre rather than to the New Testament.

What the New Testament says about Easter

We have seen how the first disciples tried to tell the story of what happened to them after Jesus had been crucified. Other Christians, when they had had a lot of time to think about it, tried to write down what it all meant.

When St Paul was writing to the church at Corinth he knew that there was an argument going on about whether the Resurrection of Christ was important or not. He had no doubts. He wrote: 'If Christ has not been raised then our preaching is in vain and your faith is in vain. If Christ has not been raised your faith is futile.' (1 Corinthians 15: 14, 17.)

Although the date of Easter is decided by the sun and the moon the dates of other festivals for Christians depend on Easter. Everything revolves around that and the event it celebrates. The power of whatever happened on that first Easter morning began the worship of Christ as God, which started a new religion and changed the world. For Christians it is the central point of history.

Towards the end of his life St Paul tried to say just what it all meant to Christians. In one of his most famous pieces of writing he wrote:

Is it Christ Jesus, who died, yes, who was raised from the dead, who is at the right hand of God, who shall intercede for us? Who shall separate us from the love of Christ? Shall tribulation, or distress, or persecution, or famine, or nakedness, or peril, or the sword?

No, in all these things we are more than conquerors through him who loved us. For I am sure that neither death nor life, nor angels, nor principalities, nor things present, nor things to come, nor powers, nor height, nor depth, nor anything else in all creation, will be able to separate us from the love of God in Christ Jesus our Lord.
(Romans 8: 33—39)

But perhaps even St Paul could not say it all in words. That is why Christians still celebrate this festival. To express what they feel they need to use all the senses, sight, smell, taste and touch, as well as sound and when they do use their voices at Easter the most common cry is simply 'Alleluia! — praise be to God'. There is more meaning yet to be discovered to this greatest of all mysteries.

THINGS TO DO

Christmas

1 Make some Christmas cards to send to (a) Christians (b) people of other religions. Find out more about why people send them.

2 Learn how to say 'Happy Christmas' in as many different languages as you can.

3 Imagine you were a slave in the days of the Roman Empire. Describe what you would do on the feast-day of saturnalia when for just one day in the year you were treated as a free person.

4 Relate a story through the eyes of one of the following characters: (a) The shepherds on the hillside (b) The Magi (c) A soldier of Herod sent to kill the infant boys.

5 Make a Christmas crib. Perhaps you could use a box for the stable, making figures from pipe-cleaners; or buy small dolls and dress them in clothes made from scraps of material. If you have no model animals, you could make them from wood or plasticine or carve them from soap.

6 Study a nativity play which includes songs and music. Or make up a nativity play of your own, perhaps to perform for your family or class.

7 Make a frieze showing the different parts of the Christmas story, or make an abstract decoration using as many different Christmas symbols as you can.

8 Make paper chains, Christmas lanterns and other decorations for your home and classroom.

9 Write down all the Christmas symbols you can think of. Divide the list into two, one list of all the symbols which are definitely Christian; the other containing all those which are connected with winter. Finally look at the winter list and decide which ones have been given some Christian meaning. Say what it is.

10 Make up your own Christmas Book. Put in it all the things you like best about Christmas, including poems and stories about Christmas, and decorate it with drawings.

11 Many people feel lonely at Christmas, especially the elderly or sick. Find out what organizations in your area help these people. Perhaps you could help, too, by visiting an old people's home or day centre.

12 Visit churches and look at their Christmas cribs. Talk to a vicar or minister about what special activities go on in the church at Christmas time.

13 Write your own Christmas carol and set it to music. Write several songs and combine them in a Christmas musical.

14 The robin is a bird we traditionally associate with Christmas, but many other birds are winter visitors. Put out food for the birds and make a note of those that visit your bird-table.

15 Discuss the suggestion that today's commercialism of Christmas is a continuation of the old pagan festival of the winter solstice and that the Christian festival only begins when the shops shut on Christmas Eve.

16 Read again the story of the Slaughter of the Innocents in Matthew 2: 13–23. Discuss whether or not you think it is an essential part of the Christmas story. Have we made the Christian Christmas too cosy and comfortable by often leaving it out? Why do you think Matthew included it?

Shrove Tuesday

1 Write a short account of what Lent is about. Explain the meaning of 'Shrove' in Shrove Tuesday and describe the reasons why, in France, it is called Mardi Gras.

2 Make pancakes using the following recipe:

RECIPE

Ingredients: One egg
100 g of flour
200 ml of milk

Method: Beat the egg into the flour. Add the milk slowly while stirring to ensure there are no lumps in the mixture. Allow to stand for five minutes.
Heat a small amount of fat in a shallow pan and pour in enough of the mixture to cover the bottom of the pan. Allow one side to brown before turning (or tossing) the pancake. The secret of good pancakes is a smooth mixture, hot fat, and keeping them thin.

---

3 Find out all you can about the history of football and about the sorts of games that were traditionally played on Shrove Tuesday.

4 Design a fancy dress for Mardi Gras and give details of the materials you would use.

5 Organize your own Mardi Gras carnival (see the film *Festival of Friendship* listed on page 107).

6 Say why you think it is that people who live in very poor conditions, even in slavery, often create the most colourful festivals.

7 Invite a local priest or minister to come and tell you about Ash Wednesday and Lent and what happens in their church.

8 Read again Chapter 4, pages 47–8. Write a short account saying what things you would give up for Lent. Say why.

9   Imagine what it would be like to be really hungry. Try to describe what it must be like to live in those parts of the world where there is little food.

10 Discover all you can about work done by organizations such as Christian Aid, Oxfam, War on Want, Save the Children Fund and others. Contact the Christian Aid organizer in your area.

Holy Week

1   One of the tasks taken most seriously at Oberammergau is that of choosing the person to play Jesus Christ in the play. The villagers try to select someone who is worthy of the part. If you were producing a passion-play who would you choose from all the people you know (male or female) and why?

2   Play a game of charades about feelings using symbolic actions. Divide into two groups. One group goes away and decides on a subject, for example 'Life', 'Rebirth', 'Victory'. Think up your own subject then mime it in front of the first group, who are allowed one guess each. Then the groups change over.

3   Read the story of Palm Sunday from the following Gospels: Mark 11:1–11; Luke 19:28–45 and Matthew 21:1–17. Write down in two columns what is the same in their descriptions and what is different.

4   Begin a scrapbook or project on 'Special Gates and Doorways'. Look for pictures. Notice special entrances to churches, schools, halls, etc., in your town or village.

5   Find out how Palm Sunday is celebrated in different local churches.

6   Write an imaginary account of the cleansing of the temple as if you were (a) a visiting pilgrim following Jesus, (b) a stall holder, (c) a priest at the temple.

7 Read the questions of Holy Week put to Jesus and taken from the Bible references given on page 63. Write down (a) each question, (b) why it was a difficult question, (c) how Jesus answered it, (d) why the answer was successful.

8 Read again the story of the widow's mite from Mark 12:41–44. Describe what would be the most difficult thing for you to give away and why.

9 Read again the account of Jesus washing the feet of his disciples in John 13:1–11. Say why you think this action has been changed into the present Maundy service. As symbols, what is the difference between washing feet and giving out money?

10 Try and attend a communion service or, better still, go to different churches. Unless you have been baptized and/or confirmed you will probably not be able to take part but you will be allowed to watch as long as you do so quietly and reverently. Afterwards write down both what you saw and what you felt.

11 Read the story of the crucifixion from one of the references given on page 70. Discuss whether or not you would tell the story to children much younger than yourself.

12 Visit a Roman Catholic church and look at the Stations of the Cross around the walls. If you arrange with the priest beforehand he will probably be glad to explain them to you.

13 Plan an imaginary Good Friday procession around your town or city. Decide where the stations or stopping points should be.

14 Organize a marbles or a skipping competition. Write down any rhymes you know which go with skipping, especially long-rope skipping, and see if you can discover what they were originally about.

15 Find out more about hot cross buns and the superstitions and stories attached to them. Find a recipe for hot cross buns and make some for Good Friday.

Easter

1 Make your own Easter egg decorations either on real egg shells, or, if that is not possible, on paper.
2 Find out as much as you can about morris dancers and what some of their dances might be about. Say why you think that the morris men start their dancing season at Easter time.
3 Look through a hymn-book and find Easter hymns. Learn to play or sing the melody of one you have not seen before.
4 Write your own Easter carol.
5 Make an 'Easter bonnet' out of bits and pieces. Organize a parade and ask someone to be the judge.
6 Write an imaginative story which begins with words, 'The hare stood all alone in the middle of the field. There was no one in sight. Not a sound could be heard. Suddenly. . .'
7 Find out all you can about local Easter customs. Your public library might be able to help.
8 Read the Easter stories in a modern version of the Bible, using the references given in Chapter 2, pages 88–91.
9 Find out all you can from an encyclopaedia about Bede and Eostre. Also look up information on Adonis.
10 Write one of the Easter stories in your own words as if you were one of the women visiting the tomb or one of the men in the other stories. Tell what you feel as well as what you see and hear.
11 Make a collage or a painting using some or all of the symbols mentioned in Chapter 3, pages 92–3.
12 Make a paschal candle for your own room or classroom. Light it for a short time every day between Easter and Ascension Day.
13 Make an Easter garden as a class or group project.
14 Make a frieze for the classroom wall putting in as many of the stories, activities and symbols associated with Easter as you can.
15 Draw a diagram to show the meaning of spring or vernal equinox.

16 Try and get hold of a record of Handel's *Messiah* and listen to the 'Hallelujah Chorus'. Discuss what the words and music together are attempting to say about Easter.

17 Compose, or write the words for a song to be part of a rock musical. The title of the song could be *Easter's the Time for a Big Celebration*.

18 Write out the words of one of the statements of St Paul given in Chapter 4, pages 98–9, perhaps as an illuminated manuscript. Then learn the words by heart.

BOOKS AND OTHER RESOURCES

Books

Bible Stories for Today: New Testament by J.G. Priestley (RMEP)
Christian Objects edited by Susan Tompkins (Christian Education Movement)
Christmas by B. Cooney (Longman)
The Easter Book by Jenny Vaughan (Macdonald)
Festivals and Customs by Norman J. Bull (RMEP)
Festive Occasions in the Primary School by Redvers Brandling (Ward Lock)
Folklore and Customs of Rural England by Margaret Baker (David & Charles)

Other Resources

Festival of Friendship – A film showing how a city primary school turned preparation for celebrating Mardi Gras into a school project. Available from Concord Video & Film Council Ltd, 201 Felixstowe Road, Ipswich, Suffolk IP3 9BJ.

Festivals – A series of audio-visual packs produced by the Regional R.E. Centre (Midlands) in conjunction with Mary Glasgow Publications. Available from Stanley Thornes Ltd, Old Station Drive, Leckhampton, Cheltenham, Glos. GL53 0DN.